Proj. 00381 1972

Our Foreign-Born Citizens

Our Foreign-Born Citizens

SIXTH EDITION

By Annie E. S. Beard

THOMAS Y. CROWELL COMPANY
NEW YORK

Published in Canada by Fitzhenry & Whiteside Limited, Toronto

MANUFACTURED IN THE UNITED STATES OF AMERICA
L.C. Card 68-17083
ISBN: 0-690-60525-0
THIRD PRINTING OF SIXTH EDITION

The University of Chicago Press has kindly given permission to reprint excerpts from Atoms in the Family *by Laura Fermi. Copyright 1954 by The University of Chicago.*

The poetry excerpts in the chapter on W. H. Auden are from The Collected Poetry of W. H. Auden, *copyright 1945 by W. H. Auden;* Letters from Iceland, *copyright 1937; and* Nones, *copyright 1939, 1946, 1947, 1949, 1950, 1951 by W. H. Auden and copyright 1950 by The Curtis Publishing Company; all are published by Random House, Inc.*

Preface

MOST Americans are immigrants or the descendants of immigrants. The American Indian alone can safely trace all the roots of his family tree back to their source in the soil of America. And scholars tell us that even the Indian probably immigrated in prehistoric times, coming into the western hemisphere over a land bridge that once connected the Americas with Asia. Unfortunately, people whose families have lived in this country for two, three, four, or more generations sometimes tend to forget these facts. They assume that length of stay has given them certain privileges—certain virtues even—which later comers cannot share. Nothing, of course, could be further from the truth. Early comers and late, all have contributed to the greatness of America, and all must share in its privileges if our country is to remain a great one.

From the time of its first printing, one of the great values of *Our Foreign-Born Citizens* has been its demonstration of the importance of the role that immigrants have played in developing our country. But since Miss Beard wrote her book there have been many more newcomers to America. And these newcomers have made important contributions, too. New industries have sprung up, and immigrants like Igor Sikorsky, Spyros Skouras, and Raymond Loewy have risen with them. Walter Gropius has fostered a new school of architecture. New leadership has been demanded by our workers, and men like Philip Murray and David Dubinsky have answered the call. Popular entertainment has been provided by people like Alfred Hitchcock. Since Miss Beard's day, too, American art has been enriched by the work of Hans Hofmann, its poetry and music by W. H. Auden and Erich Leinsdorf. And the frontiers of darkness have been pushed farther back through the efforts of Hideyo Noguchi, a Japanese-born scientist, and Enrico Fermi from Italy.

America has profited enormously from the work of her immigrants. But she has not always been uniformly just in her treatment of her benefactors. Hideyo Noguchi never became a citizen of the United States, though he wished to become one. Prejudicial laws enacted by bigoted legislators discriminated against members of his race for many years, denying them citizenship. Dr. Noguchi appears in this book because he was a great American; that he was not technically a citizen was no fault of his.

One further word must be said about Miss Beard's work. Rectifying an injustice, she brought recognition to American citizens of foreign birth whose contributions

to our country had long been overlooked. In doing so
she did a service for the immigrant and for her country.
Of course, with the passage of time new information on
some of her subjects has come to light. In some cases,
notably the chapter on Andrew Carnegie, this information has been significant enough to justify a reassessment
of the subject. But in the majority of instances I have
merely supplemented what Miss Beard had to say by
adding information which she did not have access to
when she wrote.

Contents

Contents

Our Foreign-Born Citizens

John James Audubon

THE French painter Gérard called John James Audubon "the king of ornithological painters" after seeing his wonderful life-size drawings of the birds of America. Baron Georges Cuvier, a noted French naturalist, spoke of them as "the most splendid monuments which art has erected in honor of ornithology."

The man who won this high praise was born in the Louisiana territory on May 4, 1785. His father was French and his mother was Spanish. His father, the twentieth child of a poor fisherman, set out at the early age of twelve to seek his fortune and became a sailor. Finally he was given command of a small vessel of the Imperial navy and frequently visited America. So it happened that his famous son, John James, was born there, although a few years later the child was taken to the family's home at Nantes, in France.

He spent a happy boyhood, for through his stepmother's indulgence he was not kept strictly at school but was allowed to spend much time in the woods watching the birds and gathering their nests, thus early showing the interest that became the dominant influence of his life. His father, on his return home from a voyage, finding the boy was missing the benefits of an education, sent him away to school. Among other studies he had the advantage of drawing lessons from the celebrated French painter Jacques Louis David from whom he learned how to sketch from nature. At the age of seventeen he had already made sketches of two hundred varieties of birds, but his father was disappointed in him because he did not wish to serve under Napoleon as a soldier. As an alternative to such service the boy was sent to America to look after some of his father's property at Mill Grove, near the Schuylkill Falls, Pennsylvania.

At Mill Grove he spent his time hunting, fishing, and drawing. His next door neighbor, an Englishman, had a beautiful daughter with whom he fell in love at first sight. And after an interval of a few years, Audubon married her. Both before and after his marriage various ventures into business ended disastrously. He had no aptitude for such a life and devoted himself far more assiduously to outdoor occupations, studying the habits of the birds and animals he found in the woods. His father's death brought him no financial gain, for the merchant with whom his father had deposited seventeen thousand dollars refused to hand the money over to the son until assured of his legal right to it. Meanwhile the merchant died penniless and John James never recovered any of the money due him. With a singular disregard of his own interests he transferred to his sister Rosa the estate left by his father in France.

When another business venture turned out badly, he began to paint portraits. In this he succeeded remarkably well. Soon afterward he was offered the position of curator at a museum in Cincinnati, receiving liberal compensation for his preparation of birds. He also opened a drawing-school in the city and for a while did well financially.

On October 12, 1820, Audubon started on an expedition into Mississippi, Alabama, and Florida in search of ornithological specimens. His *Journal* gives interesting descriptions of what he saw in his wanderings, and the reader is impressed with his enthusiasm over the birds and their habits.

Once he was in need of new shoes, and so also was a fellow traveler. Neither had the money to purchase them, but Audubon went to a shoemaker and offered to make portraits of the man and his wife in return for new shoes for his traveling companion and for himself. The offer was accepted and both men went on their way newly shod.

Audubon arrived in New Orleans and had no success in finding a full-time job. He received a few orders for portraits, which relieved his financial need, and he continued his work of painting birds. He also taught drawing at sixty dollars a month for half of each day. Some fourteen months later he sent for his family to join him in New Orleans. He rented a house for seventeen dollars a month and began life again with forty-two dollars. In order to educate the children Mrs. Audubon took a position as governess. Depressed in spirit because of his lack of success in earning money, her husband again went to Tennessee, paying his way on the boat with a crayon portrait of the captain and his wife. He taught drawing, music, and French in the family of a Portuguese gentleman, and drawing in a neighboring college.

After various trying experiences Audubon reached Philadelphia in the hope that he might obtain help to complete his work on birds. Through an old friend he was introduced to men of standing and influence, especially the portrait-painter Thomas Sully, who aided him greatly by giving him instruction in oil painting. With kind letters of introduction he went next to New York City but, being unsuccessful there also, he went West, mainly subsisting on bread and milk. When he arrived at Bayou Sara he found his wife had earned three thousand dollars which, with wifely generosity, she offered to him to help the publication of his book. Determined to increase the amount, he began teaching dancing to a class of sixty men and women. This brought him two thousand dollars. His determination to persevere in accomplishing the great wish of his life, in spite of the many hardships, is really remarkable.

Miraculously, at the age of forty-six, the tide of fortune turned. He went to England, where he hoped to win for his book on birds the appreciative help he had

failed to find in America. He was welcomed cordially.
From the exhibition of his pictures in Liverpool he received five hundred dollars. In Edinburgh the Royal Institution offered the use of its rooms for an exhibit that
brought in from twenty-five to seventy-five dollars a
day. He wrote to his wife:

> My success borders on the miraculous. My book is to be
> published in numbers, containing four birds in each, the
> size of life, in a style surpassing anything now existing, at
> two guineas a number. I am fêted, feasted, elected an
> honorary member of societies, making money by my ex-
> hibition and my paintings.

On March 17, 1827, he issued the prospectus of his
book, which was to cost him over one hundred thousand
dollars. But his joyous mood could not last long, for
hard work and disappointment were still ahead of him.
He visited several cities hoping to secure subscribers at
one thousand dollars each. Simultaneously he painted
pictures and then spent the evenings trying to sell them.
He said he never refused any offer made him for these
pictures. He often sold five or seven copies of one painting.

Audubon next went to Paris, where he much appreciated the acquaintance of the famous scientist, Baron
Cuvier. Among other pleasing events was the subscrip-
tion of the King of France for six copies of his *Birds of
America*. In May 1829, he returned to America, full of
delight at seeing his family again. During the next three

months, he hunted for birds and animals with which to enrich his collection for publication.

Returning to England accompanied by his wife, he found that he had been elected a Fellow of the Royal Society of London, a great honor, since only persons of recognized merit and talent were admitted. In 1830 Audubon began to prepare his *Ornithological Biography of the Birds of America.* This contained nearly a thousand pages, and he wrote industriously, a Mr. Mc-Gillivray of Edinburgh assisting him in preparing it for publication. In March 1831, his book was about completed, and he speaks in his *Journal* of spending a few days in Liverpool and "traveling on that extraordinary road, called the railway, at the rate of twenty-four miles an hour." He also says, "I have balanced my accounts with the 'Birds of America,' and the whole business is really wonderful; forty thousand dollars have passed through my hands for the completion of the first volume. Who would believe that a lonely individual who landed in England without a friend in the whole country and with only one sovereign in his pocket [when he reached London], could extricate himself from his difficulties, not by borrowing money, but by rising at four in the morning, working hard all day, and disposing of his works at a price which a common laborer would have thought little more than sufficient remuneration for his work? . . . During the four years required to bring the first volume before the world, no less than fifty of my subscribers, representing the sum of fifty-six thousand dollars, abandoned me."

Audubon felt that he must return again to America to explore for new birds to add to his book. He went to Florida and later to Labrador, where he collected one hundred and seventy-three skins of birds and studied the habits of the eider duck, loons, wild geese, etc. Returning to London twice more in 1834 and 1835, he published the second and third volumes of his *Ornithological Biography,* going again to America in 1836 for further research. Another trip to England saw the finish of his great work.

In 1839 Audubon came back to New York and bought a home on the banks of the Hudson River. He named it Minnie Land, in honor of his wife, Minnie being the Scotch word for mother and the name by which he usually addressed her. He had for many years wanted to visit the Rocky Mountains, and in 1843 he went to the Yellowstone with a party, in order to gather material for a book on the *Quadrupeds of America.* From the results of this expedition, undertaken when he was sixty years old, three volumes were published. He himself was equal only to the preparation of the first volume, his sons completing the others after his death in January, 1851.

Of John James Audubon one writer has said:

Of the naturalists of America, no one stands out in more picturesque relief than he. He undertook and accomplished one of the most gigantic tasks that has ever fallen to the lot of man to perform. For more than three-quarters of a century his splendid paintings . . . which for spirit and vigor are still unsurpassed, have been the admiration of the world. As a field naturalist he was at his best and had few equals. He was a keen observer, and possessed the rare gift of instilling into his writings the freshness of nature and the vivacity and enthusiasm of his own personality. His was a type now rarely met, combining the grace and culture of the Frenchman, with the candor, patience, and earnestness of purpose of the American.

As a pioneer in an unknown field he naturally made some mistakes, but he was always sincere and honest in presenting his convictions. Another writer said:

He has enlarged and enriched the domains of a pleasing and useful science; he has revealed to us the existence of many species of birds before unknown; he has given us more accurate information of the forms and habits of those that were known; and he has imparted to the study of natural history the grace and fascination of romance.

The National Audubon Society is a fitting monument to this lover of birds. It sustains the Audubon wardens, the minute men of the coast, whose duty it is to protect the waterfowl from destruction because of their service to humanity as the scavengers of the coast region. It maintains havens for the birds at nesting time, and in many ways protects our feathered friends.

Andrew Carnegie

IN June 1889, there appeared in the *North American Review* an article called "The Gospel of Wealth." It bore the name of Andrew Carnegie and exalted, as conditions imposed by nature, "the concentration of business, industrial and commercial, in the hands of the few, and the law of competition between these, as being not only beneficial, but essential to the progress of the race." Perhaps there was nothing strange in finding such sentiments expressed by a man whose industrial empire, which was soon to be recapitalized at 320 million dollars, was then reaping profits of 2 million a year, especially since the author had begun life as a bobbin boy in a cotton factory at $1.20 a week. But it is curious to find that this defender of inequality, who praised the virtues to be acquired through struggle, owes his reputation to philanthropy rather than pugnacity, to charity rather than industry. And the life of Andrew Carnegie is full of such curious paradoxes: a poor boy, he became fabulously wealthy; unscrupulous in business, he donated millions to philanthropic ends; a robber baron, he hated war; uneducated, he endowed seats of learning and introduced millions of people to cultural influences; a rugged individualist, he prepared the way for industry-strangling monopoly; a professed democrat, he helped to undermine democracy by concentrating power in the hands of a few.

The career of this paradoxical individual began on November 25, 1835, in the small Scottish town of Dunfermline, the town from which the king in the old ballad sends his summons to Sir Patrick Spens. The boy's father was a master weaver, the last of a long succession of skilled hand weavers of damask, who was ruined by the introduction of the power loom and the advent of the factory system. But in the faraway city of Pittsburgh, Pennsylvania, at the juncture of the Allegheny and Monongahela rivers, there were relatives, and to that industrial American city the family turned. They settled in nearby Allegheny City in 1847, and in a local cotton factory both William Carnegie and his thirteeen-year-old son Andrew found work. Andrew began as a bobbin boy, soon shifting jobs to become an engineer's assistant. The resounding title cloaked a menial task, for he merely stoked a steam boiler. But he was given an eighty-cent increase in pay. Working twelve hours a day, he was now earning two dollars a week.

One evening in 1850 when Andrew returned from work his uncle told him that a messenger boy was wanted in the Pittsburgh telegraph office. Andrew applied for the job and, despite his smallness and his imperfect knowledge of the city, he was employed. Leaving the steam boiler and the grimy cellar, he was, he says, "lifted into paradise, yes, heaven, as it seemed to me, with newspapers, pens, pencils, and sunshine about me." Moreover, he now earned two dollars and fifty cents a week.

It was while working as a messenger boy that Carnegie made his first attempt at financial organization. The boys who delivered messages were allowed to collect an extra charge of ten cents for delivery beyond a certain area. These "dime messages" were the cause of trouble among the boys, since frequent quarrels arose over the right of delivery. Young Carnegie suggested "pooling" the messages and dividing the extra money equally among the boys. His suggestion was adopted, and he was made treasurer of the pool. Thereafter, as he tells it, "Peace and good humor reigned."

Despite Andrew's solution of the problem, he was not popular with the other messenger boys. He was accused of being penurious, never spending his share of extra dimes for candy and buns as the other boys did. Moreover, he lectured the others on their extravagance. But his close ways and good manners were well thought of by the manager, who often chose Andrew to watch the office during his own absence. This extra work won him a slight raise in pay. It also provided him with an opportunity to learn telegraphy, an opportunity which he put to unexpected use one morning when an urgent message came through before the regular operator arrived for duty. Taking the message accurately, Andrew was rewarded for his diligence by being assigned as a substitute operator during another emergency. Before long he was made a regular operator at a salary of twenty-five dollars a month.

Though young Andrew had been working hard, he had not spent all of his time in the telegraph office. Through the kindness of Colonel James Anderson, who had opened his private library to Pittsburgh working boys, Carnegie was able to borrow a book a week. In later years he attributed his own benefactions in founding libraries to the example of Colonel Anderson. To the same man, who had often helped him in his selection of books, he owed his appreciation of literature, a taste, which he asserted, he "would not exchange for all the millions that were ever amassed by man." This taste proved even financially profitable to the young telegrapher, however. Reading history gave him an interest in world affairs, and he was able to earn an extra dollar a week making copies of the foreign news reports that came over his wire and distributing them to local newspapers.

Carnegie next sought to ingratiate himself with Thomas A. Scott, divisional superintendent of the Pennsylvania Railroad at Pittsburgh and, purportedly, "one of the shrewdest intriguers in the railroad business." Offered a job as railroad telegrapher and secretary to

Scott, Andrew immediately accepted. Shortly thereafter an accident occurred on one of the lines during Scott's absence. Andrew took it upon himself to order the resumption of schedules—an order that only Scott could give—in his boss's name. The order saved time for the line, but it might have cost lives. Since the episode had no serious consequences, the wily superintendent kept his "white-haired Scotch devil" with him, knowing that such unscrupulousness might prove useful. And so it did, for Carnegie later employed labor spies to compile a blacklist and break a strike for his boss.

At the age of sixteen Carnegie was given a stock-market tip by Scott. Mortgaging his now-widowed mother's home, he raised five hundred dollars for his first market speculation, and it proved to be successful. Some time later he met Thomas T. Woodruff, inventor of the first sleeping car, and through his connection with Scott, he was able to advance Woodruff's plan for the manufacture of the car. Carnegie borrowed enough money to invest $217.50 in the new sleeping car company, and in two years he was making $5,000 a year from this investment alone. Other investments followed, notably a "flyer" in some oil acreage which netted him many thousands of dollars. The young man was so delighted upon fruition of the latter scheme that he exclaimed, "Oh, I'm rich! I'm rich!"

The beginning of the Civil War found Carnegie, a professed Abolitionist, still working for Scott, who had become Assistant Secretary of War in charge of the Transportation Department, in Washington. But with the Union defeat at Bull Run and the prospect of a long war, both Scott and Carnegie left Washington. As a matter of fact, with the war increasing in severity, twenty-seven-year-old Andrew decided that he needed a vacation in Scotland. He left for Dunfermline on June 28, 1862, shortly after the costly battle of Shiloh had taken place. His stay in Scotland was prolonged by a siege of illness, but he returned to America before the end of the war and made plans for a career in industry, which was then beginning to flourish.

The significant work of Andrew Carnegie, like that of the carpetbaggers, was undertaken during the period of reconstruction. Through his connection with the railroads, he was able to see the importance of iron in industrial America. Shrewdly, he decided to abandon his other interests at the close of the Civil War and concentrate on iron. Within a few years he had organized or bought into companies that made iron bridges, rails, and locomotives. Then he moved to New York, the center of high finance, to act as salesman for his companies and as broker for numerous railroad and iron interests. His brashness had not deserted him with the acquisition of wealth, nor had he lost his ability to ingratiate himself with influential people. Soon he was making enormous commissions on various brokerage "deals" and plowing his winnings back into his iron interests.

In 1867 at the age of thirty-two, with an income of $50,000 a year, Carnegie decided that he wanted to quit business life. His ambition was to "settle in Oxford and get a thorough education, making the acquaintance of literary men." He made the following entry in his diary at this time:

> Man must have an idol—the amassing of money is one of the worst species of idolatry—no idol more debasing than the worship of money. . . . To continue much longer overwhelmed by business cares and with most of my thoughts wholly upon the way to make more money in the shortest time, must degrade me beyond hope of permanent recovery.

However, upon visiting London the young entrepreneur met the "crazy Frenchman" Bessemer, then working upon further experiments in steel. He saw the Bessemer converter in action and experienced a change of heart that resembled a religious conversion. "Jumping on the first available steamer, he rushed home" to Pittsburgh, shouting: "The day of Iron has passed—Steel is King!" A literary life at Oxford and hopes of permanent recovery from commercialism were forgotten, and Carnegie was on his way to amassing new fortunes in steel.

Carnegie's sudden vision of the new day of steel had been rather late in coming. Practical steel making had been under way in England for more than a decade before he realized its importance. In America, too, the brilliant Alexander Holley had been setting up Bessemer plants since 1865. Even Carnegie's own partner, William Coleman, had for over six years been urging him to go into steel manufacturing.

Despite his late start, however, Carnegie was soon turning out more Bessemer steel than all the other American mills combined. Enjoying a high protective duty which eliminated British competition, being favorably located for production, and already dominating the iron industry, Carnegie determined to supply steel to the expanding country in enormous quantities. The plant which he built in 1875, on Braddock's battlefield on the banks of the Monongahela, was the largest and most elaborate steel plant in the country. A capital investment of over a million dollars made competition prohibitively costly and restricted it to a limited number of firms. And Carnegie was quick to take advantage of hard times by buying up or ruining his rivals. Underselling opponents until he had forced them out of business and then raising his prices again, he soon became known as the "pirate" of the steel industry.

Carnegie was as thoroughly hated and feared by his own working force as by rival industrialists whom he had ruined. His labor policy was, in the words of a historian of the period, "thoroughly bad." By a system of "unfriendly competition" for which he became infamous in the industry, he forced his managers and supervisors to get maximum production from his laborers for very little pay. Unionism was inhibited. The "lockout" was frequently employed in disputes. Accidents were common, for few safety precautions were taken. One of his most valuable technical aides, Captain "Billy" Jones, a man whose industrial know-how amounted to genius, met a horrible death in an explosion of molten metal in one of the plants. This was a serious blow to Carnegie, for he himself had but the scantiest knowledge of the techniques of steel production and he had to depend upon his skilled assistants. But even these underlings were as shabbily treated as his workers. Whenever he was informed (in Pittsburgh, New York, Scotland, or wherever his scattered interests took him) of a production peak in one of his plants, Carnegie would telegraph: "Congratulations! Why not do it every week?" Or, told that one of his furnaces had broken all records, he would ask: "What were the other ten furnaces doing?"

Though Carnegie soon succeeded in dominating the steel industry through these methods, he still feared three giant antagonists. The first of these with whom he came to grips was Henry Clay Frick, who, with a monopoly of coal lands, controlled the production of coke. Carnegie knew that he "could not get on without a supply of the fuel essential to the smelting of pig iron" and, rather than risk a war with the millionaire baron of coke, he joined forces with him. In 1889 Frick became general manager, under Carnegie, of the tremendous combine formed from the two industries.

John D. Rockefeller, privately referred to as "Reck a fellow" by Carnegie, was another thorn in the Scotsman's side. He had acquired, in addition to his oil lands, large sections of the Mesabi Range, the richest ore lands in the world. Carnegie feared a "squeeze" on another essential raw material, and he hastily bought some acreage in the Range to use as a bargaining lever. Then he began to bargain with "my dear fellow millionaire," as he addressed his rival directly. When negotiations were completed Carnegie held, by lease or ownership, two thirds of the Mesabi deposits. The Carnegie companies also "owned and controlled mines producing 6,000,000 tons of ore annually; 40,000 acres of coal land and 12,000 coke ovens; steamship lines for transporting ore to Lake Erie ports; docks for handling ore and coal and a railroad from Lake Erie to Pittsburgh; 70,000 acres of natural gas territory with 200 miles of pipe line; nineteen blast furnaces and five steel mills producing and finishing 3,250,000 tons of steel annually."

But, even when entrenched behind the massive vertical wall of his combine, Carnegie was still vulnerable. J. P. Morgan, the banker, was busily amalgamating metal trusts and railroads in a network of interlocking directorates that would eventually be capable of undermining any company, no matter how large. Carnegie began to feel the pinch when the Pennsylvania Railroad suddenly doubled his freight rates. He determined to fight, and he was ready to use the millions he held in reserve to build a new railroad and cut his way to the sea. Then he would undertake a steel war in earnest, wrecking his opponents and himself, if necessary. The master banker, Morgan, saw his cunningly fabricated empire tottering and he decided to stop the war by buying Carnegie out. In 1901 Carnegie sold his companies to J. P. Morgan for $492,000,000. The price, according to Morgan, "made Carnegie the richest man in the world." It also made U. S. Steel, the corporation Morgan formed with his new holdings, the largest and most powerful monopoly in America.

No longer concerned with "the way to make more money in the shortest possible time," the richest man in the world now sought to perpetuate his memory through the distribution of some of his uncountable millions of dollars. His first charitable act was to establish a fund to be used in caring for aged employees who had worn out their lives in his service. Then, having derived all the education he had from reading, he sought to make books available to greater numbers of people, contributing close to $60,000,000 to public libraries. He endowed the Carnegie Institute of Washington, D.C., with $25,000,000 "to encourage . . . research and discovery, and the application of knowledge to the improvement of mankind." In Pittsburgh, where he had made his fortune, Carnegie spent $28,000,000 on an institute which embraced a library, a museum, a picture gallery, and the Carnegie School of Technology. The Carnegie Corporation of New York received $125,000,000 for the advancement of education and research. Such widely separated and diverse institutions as the University of St. Andrews in Scotland and the Mount Wilson Observatory in California benefited by his gifts. And he donated money for a variety of causes ranging from a pension fund for aged university professors to contributions for church organs. In all he distributed something over $350,000,000.

Of course, Andrew Carnegie deserves praise for his gifts. Though people who knew him asserted that he "never gave anything without the requirement that his name be attached to the gift," the men and women who have read in the libraries, studied in the schools, or worked in the laboratories that Carnegie endowed have profited no less fully. Nevertheless, our praise for the bringer of such gifts must be qualified by our knowledge of the man and of the spirit in which he gave. And the paradoxical Carnegie seems to have given millions from a variety of contradictory reasons. Gratitude, patriotism, love for humanity doubtless influenced him in some degree. But in an age when Rockefeller, Morgan, Mellon, and Frick were distributing millions to sweeten their unsavory reputations and enshrine their memories, philanthropy was a competitive business which Andrew Carnegie could hardly resist. Since his own reputation needed some sweetening, his gifts were bound to be large. It has been pointed out, moreover, that "the distribution of immense charities, no less than sumptuary extravagance" is a form of "conspicuous consumption" designed to call attention to "successful predatory aggression." And few were more successful in this sphere than Andrew Carnegie.

Carnegie died in 1919. He is remembered, as he wished to be, through the numerous charities which he established. His role as a baron of steel is almost forgotten now, concealed behind the mask of the philanthropist that he donned in his later years. Perhaps this is the greatest paradox of his contradictory career. As Eugene Schneider, head of the Creusot Steel Works in France, said of him after his death: "He gave a little recognized contribution to the progress of the world: He popularized steel, and showed that cheap steel is one of the greatest gifts ever produced for mankind."

John Muir

I N 1838 among the wilds of Scotland, at Dunbar by the stormy North Sea, a boy was born who was always to delight in nature and who even in his old age would climb almost inaccessible mountains and travel long journeys into unfrequented places. John Muir was the eldest son of hard-working Scottish people and had few pleasures. He was sent to school when he was only three years old, his grandfather having previously taught him the letters of the alphabet from the street signs opposite his home.

School was not a place of enjoyment for John, for, like many another boy, he was mischievous and venturesome and paid the penalty by having frequent thrashings. Between the ages of seven and eight he left the "Auld Davel Brae Schule" for the grammar school. Here he had three lessons a day in Latin, three in French, and as many in English, in addition to spelling, arithmetic, history, and geography. At home his father made him learn so many verses of the Bible that when he was eleven years old he knew by heart three quarters of the Old Testament and all of the New Testament. As he himself quaintly puts it: "By sore flesh I was able to recite the New Testament from the beginning to the end without a single stop, for the grand, simple, all-sufficient Scotch discovery had been made that there was a close connection between the skin and the memory, and that irritation of the skin excited the memory to any required degree."

Boys of today would surely think themselves badly treated if they were given the meals John Muir and his brothers and sisters had. For breakfast they had oatmeal porridge with a little milk or molasses. Dinner consisted usually of vegetable broth, a small piece of boiled mutton, and barley scone. For tea they were given half a slice of white bread without butter, barley scone, and a drink called "content," which was simply warm water with a little milk and sugar. For supper they had a boiled potato and barley scone. The only fire for the whole house was in the little kitchen stove, the firebox of which was eight inches long and eight inches in width and depth.

Into the monotony of this life came one day a joyous surprise when Father Muir said, "Bairns, you needna learn your lessons the nicht, for we're gaen to America the morn." For many years after that John's home was at Kingston, near Fort Winnebago, Wisconsin. The heavy burden of clearing and plowing the land fell on him, although he was only twelve years old. One of his particularly hard experiences was the digging of the well, into which he was lowered every morning at sunrise, and there spent the day chiseling away the hard rock, except for a short interval at noon. This slow method occupied many months and was a great trial to a boy who loved outdoor life. When he had reached a depth of eighty feet he nearly lost his life by being overcome with gas. In that pioneer existence there was much hardship. At one time when he was sick with the mumps he was kept at work in the harvest field even though he fainted more than once. For several weeks he was ill with pneumonia, but he had to struggle through without any aid from a doctor.

At fifteen years of age John Muir became eager for an education. He borrowed such books as he could get and, because his father would not let him stay up at night, he rose at one o'clock every morning, studying in the cellar as the warmest place in the cold winter days. He developed a talent for invention, making his own tools out of the materials at hand. He made a fine saw out of strips of steel from old corsets; bradawls, punches, and a pair of compasses from wire and old files. He constructed a timekeeper which indicated the days of the month and of the week as well as the hours. One of his clocks kept good time for fifty years. He also built a self-setting sawmill and an automatic contrivance for feeding horses at a required hour.

When he was twenty-one Muir left home, with only fifteen dollars in his pocket. He went to the State Fair and exhibited his inventions, which elicited much wonder and interest. Soon after, he enrolled at the University of Wisconsin. He had not attended school since he had left Scotland except for two months in a district school, but after a few weeks in the preparatory department he qualified as a freshman. He spent four years at the university. In his book, *My Boyhood and Youth,* he says: "I earned enough during summer vacations to pay thirty-two dollars a year for instruction, my books, acids, retorts, glass tubes, etc. I had to cut down expenses for board to half a dollar a week."

During this period he invented an apparatus which, when attached to his bed, not only awakened him at a definite hour but simultaneously lighted a lamp. After so many minutes allotted for dressing, a book was pushed up from a rack below the top of his desk, thrown open, and allowed to remain there a certain number of minutes. Then the machinery closed the book, dropped it back into its place, and moved the rack forward with the next book required.

Having completed his work at the university, John Muir started on a trip to Canada on foot. He worked in a mill there for a year, improving its machinery and inventing appliances. Then he went to Indianapolis and in a carriage and wagon factory was offered the position of foreman with a prospective partnership. But one of his eyes was injured in an accident, and after several weeks of confinement in a dark room he decided "to get away into the flowery wilderness to enjoy and lay in a large stock of God's wild beauty before the coming on of the time of darkness." He therefore went on foot on a botanizing tour to Cedar Keys on the Gulf of Mexico, and later he traveled to Cuba. In 1868 he went to California. There in the Yosemite he lived for many years, occasionally taking trips to still wilder places. He climbed the most inaccessible mountains and discovered some sixty-five glaciers. One of his remarkable feats was crawling along a three-inch ledge to the brink of the 1600-foot plunge of the Upper Yosemite creek to listen, as he said, "to the sublime psalm of the falls."

In 1879 he went to Alaska and, while there, he had an adventure which revealed the indomitable character of the man. Mr. Muir and his friend, S. Hall Young, were together on a mountain-climbing expedition. Mr. Young's book, *Alaska Days with John Muir,* tells us:

> Then Muir began to slide up that mountain. A deerlope over the smoother slopes, a sure instinct for the easiest way into a rocky fortress, an instant and unerring attack, a serpent glide up the steep; eye, hand, and foot all dynamically connected, with no appearance of weight to his body . . . . Fifteen years of enthusiastic study in the Sierras had given him preëminence over the ordinary climber . . . . No Swiss guide was ever wiser in the habits of glaciers than Muir . . . . Not an instant when both feet and hands were not in play; often elbows, knees, thighs, upper arms, and even chin must grip and hold. Clambering up a steep slope, crawling under an over-

hanging rock, spreading out like a flying squirrel, and edging along an inch-wide projection while fingers clasped knobs above the head, bending about sharp angles, pulling up smooth rock faces by sheer strength of arm, and chinning over the edge, leaping fissures, sliding flat around a dangerous rock breast, testing crumbling spurs before risking his weight, always going up, up, no hesitation, no pause—that was Muir.

While climbing Mr. Young met with an accident which deprived him of the use of his arms, both shoulders being dislocated. He was practically helpless, but Mr. Muir was equal to the occasion, climbing over glaciers and down the steepest crags, supporting his friend. It took all night to do it, but he succeeded. The story is a thrilling one. It concludes thus:

Sometimes he would pack me for a short distance on his back. Again taking me by the wrist he would swing me down to a lower level before descending himself. Holding my collar by his teeth as a panther her cub, and clinging like a squirrel to a tree, he climbed with me straight up ten or twelve feet, with only the help of my ironshod feet scrambling on the rock. All night this man of steel and lightning worked, never resting a minute, doing the work of three men, always cheery, full of joke and anecdote, inspiring me with his own indomitable spirit. He gave heart to me.

In one of his climbing expeditions Muir suddenly found the ground under him slipping. Instantly he threw himself on his back, spread out both arms, and so took a ride on an avalanche.

Muir was a great traveler, going in 1903 and 1914 to Europe, the Caucasus, Siberia, Japan, China, India, Egypt, Australia, and New Zealand for botanical study, and even at the age of seventy-three making a trip to the wilderness on the Amazon River and then to the jungles of Africa. But it is to his love for and investigations in the Yosemite that we are indebted to him. Largely because of his earnest and persistent efforts Yosemite, one of our most noted and wonderful parks, was made a national reserve in 1890. It is thirty-six miles in length and forty-eight in breadth. The Yosemite Valley lies in the heart of it. It includes two rivers, innumerable lakes and waterfalls, forests, ice-sculptured canyons, and mountains twelve thousand feet high. In his book, *The Yosemite,* Muir describes the wonders and beauty of this marvelous region. Among his other works are *Mountains of California, Our National Parks, My First Summer in the Sierra,* and many magazine articles. In each of his writings one glimpses the far-reaching knowledge of nature and animal life that he had acquired.

In the spring of 1880 Mr. Muir married Miss Louise Strenzel, daughter of a Polish physician who had arrived in California in 1847. Muir had a happy home, but much as he loved it and his friends, he loved nature more ardently. His devotion to it was the master passion of his life, and he himself recognized that he was "hopelessly and forever a mountaineer." "Few have loved beauty as I have, enough to forego so much to attain it." His home was a ranch forty miles from San Francisco. As soon as his vineyard was ready for the summer he would go to his loved mountains, where for three months he enjoyed every moment, living mainly on bread and tea. He fairly reveled in an earthquake that he might see the changes wrought by such a convulsion of nature. He would climb to the top of swaying branches to feel the pulsing of the heart of a storm. After these experiences he used to say, "We have met with God." Many scientists of his day said he was the greatest authority on glacial action the world has known. To the largest glacier (one in Alaska) Muir's name has been given. When he discovered it, it was fully a mile and a half in width and the perpendicular face of it towered four to seven hundred feet above the water.

A writer said of him:

Muir was Scotch to the backbone, yet America claims him as her own, so earnestly has he studied our trees, so closely is he identified with the wonders of the great West, so loyally has he labored to preserve our natural beauties when from time to time there have been those of our countrymen who would have wrested them from us. A mighty Alaskan glacier bears his name, a noble forest of California redwoods—Muir Woods—and it is likewise fitting that a little mountain daisy is his namesake, [for he would speak of a tiny fern as] one of the bonnies of our Father's bairns.

Alexander Graham Bell

"IT talks!" exclaimed Dom Pedro, Emperor of Brazil, when at the Centennial Exposition in Philadelphia in 1876 he took up a telephone receiver and put it to his ear. Then Lord Kelvin, electrical scientist of the first rank and engineer of the Atlantic cable, took his turn at the strange new instrument. "It does speak," he said. "It is the most wonderful thing I have seen in America." And so one after another notable man listened and was astonished. Thus the telephone made its first public appearance. It was the most dramatic event of the exposition which displayed many remarkable inventions.

The man who had invented this marvelous instrument was Alexander Graham Bell, who was born in Edinburgh, Scotland, on March 1, 1847. He was educated at the Royal High School of his native city and in London. But his relatives had the largest share in preparing him for his success in life. Grandfather, uncle, father, and two brothers had all specialized in the study of the laws of speech and sound and had taught and written on that subject. Through them he secured knowledge that was of great help to him in his discovery of the principle of the telephone. It was in London, soon after he reached the age of twenty-one, that his interest in scientific discovery was first aroused. Experiments were then being conducted with electromagnets and the vibrations they produced in tuning-forks.

But his progress was hindered by illness. Tuberculosis caused the death of two brothers, and he himself was threatened with the same dread disease. In hope of averting the danger, he and his father and mother left Scotland for Canada, where at Brantford he fortunately succeeded in overcoming the trouble. Meanwhile he taught a tribe of Mohawk Indians a sign language invented by his father and called "Visible Speech," each letter representing a certain action of the lips and tongue. He had previously, in London, been particularly successful in using it to teach deaf-mutes to talk. He was offered five hundred dollars by the Board of Education of Boston to introduce the system in a school for deaf-mutes. Alexander Bell gladly accepted, and his teaching met with such success that he won a professorship in Boston University and also started a school of vocal physiology which proved profitable.

At the end of two years he found opportunity to carry on his experiments in the home of a deaf-mute pupil in Salem. The father of the boy, Thomas Sanders, became deeply interested and eventually was closely associated with the development of Bell's great invention, paying practically all expenses. Gardiner G. Hubbard, the father of another deaf-mute pupil, was a well-known Boston lawyer, and he too co-operated in carrying out Bell's plans. Hubbard's daughter Mabel became the wife of the young inventor four years later, and was very helpful to him. But for the assistance of these two men it may have been impossible for Bell to succeed, for he had given up his professorship and his school in order to use his time for experiments. He was convinced that it would be possible to construct an instrument that would actually convey the sound of the human voice, and patiently he toiled by day and by night to find the principle on which it could be done.

At the suggestion of Dr. Clarence Blake, he experimented with a real ear cut from the head of a dead man. From that he conceived the idea of a telephone formed of two disks, like eardrums, far apart and connected by an electrified wire to catch the vibrations of sound at one end and reproduce them at the other. It was on an afternoon in June 1875 that Bell caught the first faint sound over the wire, but more patient study and effort had to be made before words were audible. At last, on March 10, 1876, to the almost wild delight of Bell and his assistant, Thomas Watson, the words, "Watson, come here, I want you," spoken by Bell in a room up three flights of stairs, at 109 Court Street, Boston, were heard distinctly by Watson in the basement. On his twenty-ninth birthday Bell received the patent securing his rights as inventor of the telephone.

With the exception of the few scientific men who heard it at the Centennial Exposition, no one put any faith in what Lord Kelvin described as "the greatest marvel yet achieved by the electric telegraph." Men of business said, "It is only a scientific toy; it can never be a practical necessity." It seemed so absurd to speak into a tube or box that Bell was ridiculed as "a crank who says he can talk through a wire." Yet so confident was the young inventor of the ultimate results of his discovery, that in a public address at Kensington, England, in 1878, he said:

> It is conceivable that cables of telephone wires could be laid underground or suspended overhead, connecting up by branch wires private dwellings, country houses, shops, manufacturing establishments, etc., and also connecting cities and towns and various places throughout the country. I am aware that such ideas may appear to you utopian and out of place, but I believe that such a scheme will be the ultimate result of the introduction of the telephone to the public.

His faith has been abundantly justified.

The Bell telephone as first exhibited was simply an old cigar-box and two hundred feet of wire, with a magnet from a toy fishpond, but it demonstrated the possibility of making the human voice audible to a person at a distance and out of sight. On October 9, 1876, the first conversation between two places was conducted over a wire two miles long, from Boston to Cambridge, Massachusetts. The actual words spoken and heard were published in the *Boston Advertiser* of October 19, and a little later the *Boston Globe* reported a lecture delivered in Salem and transmitted by telephone over a space of sixteen miles. In 1880 there was speech over a wire forty miles long, from Boston to Providence; and in 1885 a long-distance line was built from New York to Philadelphia; and in 1893 one from New York to Chicago. In 1896 the Rocky Mountain Bell Company had erected a seventy-thousand-mile system for the far West.

But before all this happened many disappointments and discouraging experiences had come to the men who had so persistently believed in, and worked for, the great discovery. For a long time it was almost impossible to persuade businessmen that the telephone could be of practical use to them. Then the Western Union Telegraph Company realized that it had a competitor and proceeded to fight it with all the means at its command. It induced Thomas Edison, Amos Dolbear, and Elisha Gray to invent an instrument which it advertised as the only original telephone. This action stimulated interest, and capitalists began to take hold of Bell's patents, organizing a company to develop the business in New England. Mr. Theodore Vail was made general manager, and he started to create a national telephone system. For seventeen months after Bell's invention was known no one disputed his claim, but as its value began to be appreciated other claimants appeared, and the Bell company had to engage in a patent war that continued for eleven years and included six hundred lawsuits. At last, in 1879, the Western Union acknowledged it could not prove its case, admitted that Bell was the original inventor of the telephone and that his patents were valid.

"Every telephone in the world is still made on the plan that Bell discovered. In the actual making of it there was no one with Bell or before him. He invented it first and alone." Others have made it more perfect and useful, until today "a telephone on a desk, instead of being the simple device first in use, contains no less than one hundred and thirty pieces, with a salt-spoonful of glistening granules of carbon."

After years of struggle and hardship, success came rapidly. Bell and the men who had helped him during those years of poverty, one after the other, sold out their interests in the telephone company and became millionaires. Mr. Bell himself refused an offer of ten thousand dollars a year to be the chief inventor of the company, saying he "could not invent to order." He had a handsome house in Washington and a summer home of seven hundred acres at Cape Breton, Nova Scotia, where he devoted his time to researches for the benefit of the human race. He invented the photophone and the induction balance. Men on battlefields and in hospitals have been grateful to him for his invention of the telephone-probe for the painless detection of bullets in the human body. For this he was given the honorary degree of M.D. by the University of Heidelberg. The Emperor of Japan bestowed on him the order of the Rising Sun. The Royal Society of Great Britain and the Society of Fine Arts of London gave him medals. The Government of France made him an officer of the Legion of Honor and awarded him the Volta prize of fifty thousand francs. He devoted this gift to the establishment and endowment of the Volta Bureau in Washington, for the "increase and diffusion of knowledge relating to the deaf." He also founded the American Association to Promote the Teaching of Speech to the Deaf, to which he contributed two hundred and fifty thousand dollars.

Rarely does any man within his own lifetime see such an extensive and wonderful development of the product of his own brain and hand as Alexander Graham Bell witnessed before he died in 1922. It is one of the marvels of our age.

The Bell telephone secured its first million dollars of capital in 1879; its first million dollars of earning in 1882; its first million dollars of dividends in 1884; its first million dollars of surplus in 1885. It began to send a million messages a day in 1888; strung its first million miles of wire by 1900, and installed its first million telephones by 1898. At the end of 1921 there were 13,380,-000 Bell stations in the United States, with a total of twelve billion calls for that year.

In 1927 only five years after Bell's death, the first transoceanic telephone conversation took place, between New York and London. And on April 25, 1935, Walter

S. Gifford of the Bell System talked to Theodore Miller, in the next room, on a round-the-world phone circuit stretching from New York to London, Amsterdam, Bandoeng (Java), San Francisco, and back to New York. Telephoning, meanwhile, was fast becoming a universal practice. By 1951, the seventy-fifth anniversary of the invention of the telephone, there were nearly seventy-five million phones in service throughout the world.

At the National Geographic Society dinner in Washington, D.C., on March 7, 1916, U. N. Bethell, senior vice president of the American Telephone Company, proposed a toast to "the foremost figure in the creation of this American art, that distinguished American, Dr. Alexander Graham Bell, of Scotland. We all know, though, that Dr. Bell is an American as much as any Pilgrim Father ever was. Americans of his type, who could not control the accident of birth, have helped to transform a wilderness into sovereign states, and to create great industries, important cities, vast empires, and all that sort of thing. They are proud of America and America is proud of them."

Of the wonders of the modern world the telephone ranks high on the list, and its inventor will always be regarded as one of the greatest benefactors of mankind. Dr. Bell died in 1922, full of years and honors.

Joseph Pulitzer

JOSEPH Pulitzer arrived in the United States in 1864, at the age of seventeen. He was born in Mako, Hungary, the son of an Irish mother and a Hungarian-Jewish father. Upon the death of his father, Joseph decided not to be a burden to his mother and therefore attempted to enter the army. He was rejected, however, because of a defect in one eye. Still cherishing the idea of a military life he started for the United States. He was practically penniless when he landed in Boston, and he could speak only a few words of English.

He met a fellow countryman who had just enlisted in a German cavalry regiment being raised in New York City. The unit would take part in the Civil War, and Joseph decided to join it. He served until the end of the conflict.

Joseph, full of fire and energy, was always ready to take the part of the weak and helpless. One day he could not endure seeing the brutal treatment of a fellow soldier and, without regard to army discipline, he dared to knock down the officer who was inflicting it. Of course this action involved him in trouble, and he was arrested and imprisoned to await court-martial. Meanwhile, an old general who was very fond of a good game of chess heard that this young Hungarian was a clever player. He sent for him and the two spent many hours playing chess. The general became interested in the young man, quickly discovering that he had a bright mind. Fortunately for Joseph, his new friend obtained his release.

After the army was demobilized, Joseph had several hard experiences. One night, having no other place to sleep, he chose to stay in the public park, unaware that this was not permitted. When the policeman ordered him to move on he did so, until he came to French's Hotel, in Park Row. A man in charge of the furnace told him he might sleep in the furnace-room. Before the night was over, however, he was again sent on his way by another man who later came on duty. This curious episode has the flavor of a fairy tale, for in after years Joseph Pulitzer became owner of that very building.

Soon after this adventure he decided to go West. What little money he had took him as far as East St. Louis, Illinois. He desired to cross the Mississippi but could not pay the ferryboat fare, so he offered to serve as fireman on the ferry. He pleased the captain so well that he continued to work at that task until he later secured a place as stevedore on the St. Louis wharves. He filled various positions but he was frequently handicapped by his defective eyesight.

A dangerous and hard task was given him by a St. Louis man. The charter of the St. Louis & San Francisco Railroad had to be recorded in every county of the state, and the papers in the case had to be filed with the clerk of each county. Missouri was at this time infested with bushwhackers, outlaws, and the trip was a risky undertaking for any man. Joseph was entirely ignorant of the conditions and eagerly started out on horseback. He completed his task and returned safely with worthwhile knowledge, which no other man then possessed, of every county in the state. Real estate men found the information he could give them of great value.

Even during his hard experiences he had been a great reader, and he now began to study law. In 1868, four years after he had landed in this country, he was admitted to the bar. Ambitious and full of energy as he was, he soon found that life as a young lawyer was altogether too tame for him. Gladly, therefore, he accepted the post of reporter on the *Westliche Post,* a daily newspaper of which Carl Schurz was at that time the editor. So well did Mr. Pulitzer succeed in this new undertaking that before long he became managing editor and obtained a proprietary interest in the paper. He was never afraid of anyone's opinion and never hesitated to say what he believed.

The tide of fortune had now definitely turned for Joseph Pulitzer. He had found what he could do successfully, the work which later brought him fame and riches.

In 1869 he was elected a member of the Missouri Legislature, and in 1874 to the State Constitutional Convention. In 1872 he was a delegate to the Cincinnati Convention, which nominated Horace Greeley to the presidency, and in 1880 he was a member of the platform committee of the Democratic National Convention.

In 1878 he founded the *Post Dispatch* by buying the *Dispatch* and uniting it with the *Evening Post*. This brought him a yearly income of $150,000. He was now thirty-six years old, and he decided to go to Europe for study and rest. But just then he learned that the New York *World* was for sale and, despite the warnings of his physician that health and eyesight might be sacrificed if he did not rest, the temptation was too great to be resisted. In the twenty-three years of its existence the *World* had not been much of a success, but Mr. Pulitzer soon made a change. With all the energy at his command he worked until he made it one of the leading papers of the country.

He has been called "a great journalistic force whether for good or evil." Unquestionably he had high ideals. The following words expressed his conception of a great newspaper:

An institution which should always fight for progress and reform; never tolerate injustice or corruption; always fight demagogues of all parties; never belong to any party; always oppose privileged and public plunder; never lack sympathy with the poor; always remain devoted to the public welfare; never be afraid to attack wrong.

Unfortunately he, like many another man, did not always live up to his ideals; he permitted a notable disregard for truth in the news columns of the *World*. He also at times failed to observe the rights of privacy in his eagerness to obtain information that would attract popular attention. However, the paper was frequently public-spirited in its editorials. In relation to a proposed government bond issued in 1893 he demanded that it be thrown open to the people at large at its real value, instead of being handed to a group of financiers who could reap a large profit and thus rob the government. To prove his honesty of purpose he offered a million dollars in gold for the bonds. He succeeded in his aim, for the public was given fair opportunity to purchase the bonds. Mr. Pulitizer did loyally live up to his ideals in regard to fighting against special rights and special classes and as champion of the oppressed. He insisted always upon liberty being a reality and not merely a name. Even an advertiser who paid a big price for his pages was not allowed to influence the editorial policy in the slightest degree.

As he had long expected, he was finally stricken with blindness, but his activity and energy did not lessen. His health by this time was broken and he suffered so greatly that he was compelled to live away from his family and friends much of the time, mainly on his yacht, for there he could secure the quiet he needed. He had three secretaries, whose duty it was to keep him fully posted as to what was happening all over the world. At breakfast they had to furnish him with a review of new books, plays, music, and art. At lunch they were expected to supply descriptions of important persons and events. He was continually absorbing knowledge and then dictating material for his paper or sending cablegrams to the office. Thus for years did he wonderfully control and really edit the *World,* although he rarely entered its offices.

In his adopted country Mr. Pulitzer had made millions of dollars and, while he was generous with his family and those who had served him, he was anxious to benefit his fellow citizens. He gave Columbia University two million dollars to establish a school of journalism, so that men and women writers might have special training for their work. This school has attracted worldwide attention and approval. He also provided the Pulitzer Scholarship Fund of $250,000 and funds for the support of the three graduates of the school who passed examinations with the highest honors. The money allowed them to spend a year in Europe studying political, social, and economic conditions. In all his planning for the School of Journalism, he said, his chief end in view was the welfare of the Republic.

He left an annual prize of a gold medal to be given for the most disinterested and meritorious public service rendered by any American newspaper during the year, and an annual prize of one thousand dollars to be awarded for an American novel depicting the wholesome atmosphere of American life and the highest standard of American manhood and womanhood.

To the Metropolitan Museum of Art in New York City he bequeathed $500,000, and to the Philharmonic Society a like sum.

Joseph Pulitzer died in 1911.

Augustus St. Gaudens

"You can do anything you please; it's the way you do it that makes the difference." That significant saying of Augustus St. Gaudens was well proved in all his work, for he was never satisfied until he had made it as nearly perfect as possible. When he was thirteen years old he was apprenticed to a cameo cutter and worked very hard all day at a monotonous, wearisome task. At the same time he devoted his evenings to the study of drawing in the free classes at the Cooper Institute. "I became a terrific worker," he said, toiling every night until eleven o'clock, after the classes were over. "Indeed, I became so exhausted with the confining work of cameo cutting by day and drawing by night, that in the morning Mother literally dragged me out of bed, pushed me over to the washstand, where I gave myself a cat's lick somehow or other, drove me to the table, administering breakfast, and tumbled me downstairs out into the street, where I awoke."

Augustus St. Gaudens' father was French, his mother Irish, and he inherited from them a love of the beautiful. Yet he was essentially American both in his way of thinking and in his art. He was born in Dublin in 1848 and was brought to this country in the same year. In New York City his father, Bernard St. Gaudens, opened a shop where he continued his trade of making French boots and shoes. He had the wisdom to ask his son, Augustus, what kind of work he preferred to do when, at the age of thirteen, he had to quit school. The boy said that he would like to do something which would help him to become an artist, and so he took a position as apprentice to a French cameo cutter named Avet. Under the control of this violent-tempered man Augustus had a hard time for a few years. Then in a fit of anger Avet discharged the boy, who at once went home and told his father what had occurred. When Avet came to the house a few minutes later to get Augustus to return, the boy refused to go with him. His father, who had not realized what sort of man his son had been working for, approved of the boy's decision. Later he helped his son find employment with another cameo cutter, Jules Brethon, a man of very different disposition. St. Gaudens' evenings were now spent at the National Academy of Design instead of at the Cooper Institute.

In 1867 his father offered Augustus a steerage passage to Europe, and the young man arrived in Paris with $100 saved from his wages. There, earning his living by cameo cutting in the afternoons, he devoted his mornings and evenings to study at the Petite École and, later, under the sculptor François Jouffroy at the École des Beaux Arts.

When in 1870 war was declared between France and Prussia St. Gaudens wanted to enlist on the side of France. But a pleading letter from his mother changed his mind, and he went to Rome. He produced his first statue there—that of Hiawatha "pondering, musing on the welfare of his people"—but it was only through orders for portraits given him by an American, Montgomery Gibbs, that he was able to secure enough money to have the figure cast. Back in New York for a brief period he did not at first find it easy to get worthwhile commissions, but an order for a bust of the well-known statesman William M. Evarts encouraged him.

After another visit to Rome, he returned again to the United States in 1875 and for a time had to take up teaching as a livelihood. A fortunate thing happened when he came in touch with the artist, John La Farge, for he said himself that the intimacy between them spurred him to higher endeavor. Good luck followed. The governor of New York secured for him the order for a statue of Admiral Farragut. It certainly was a triumph, for five of the committee voted to give the commission to a sculptor of high distinction, and St. Gaudens won by only one vote. Mr. La Farge also commissioned him to execute some bas-reliefs for St. Thomas Church, New York. In 1887 St. Gaudens helped to found the Society of American Artists. This Society was important, reflecting as it did a vital change in American sculpture and painting, which hitherto had been very conventional in style.

He married shortly thereafter, and he and his wife started again for Paris. For three years he worked on the bas-reliefs, which when sent to Mr. La Farge were said by him to be "a living work of art." The Farragut statue was also completed, and then St. Gaudens returned to New York. In his studio he gathered about him a circle of men who became admirers and life-long friends. Among the group were Stanford White, Charles F. McKim, H. H. Richardson, John La Farge, and others. While the result of his foreign studies was evident in his work, he used his training skillfully, establishing a distinctive American style. He was the first artist to lead sculpture away from an imitation of the classic Greek forms. His Farragut statue is a "figure instinct at every point with the energy and strength of a man fronting perils in the open air amid great winds and under a vast sky."

His medallion work was most charming, very delicate and beautiful. The Robert Louis Stevenson medallion in St. Giles' Church, Edinburgh, is one of the finest examples. "He delighted in giving a clear, even forcible impression of the personality before him. It is portraiture for the sake of truth and beauty, not for the sake of technique."

Fourteen years of his life were given largely to the modeling of the monument to Robert Gould Shaw in Boston. There were times when he dropped work on it for the fulfillment of many other commissions; at other times he worked arduously upon a high scaffolding in the hot summers, seriously injuring his health. This monument is generally considered to be one of his greatest works in imaginative power, skill of composition, and perfection of technical detail. It was characteristic of St. Gaudens to spare himself no pains if thereby he might improve his work. Shaw had been a young Bostonian, "killed in action while leading his regiment—the 54th Massachusetts—of colored men led by white officers. Across the relief march the troops to the rhythm of the drum beat; there is a martial animation, but in the faces is the tense look of anticipation of the impending battle. Occupying the center of the panel, Shaw rides beside his men, an expression of sadness on his face. Above, floats a figure to which the artist gave no name, but which his interpreters have called Fame and Death."

St. Gauden's statue of Abraham Lincoln in Chicago is universally beloved, for it reveals the very soul of the great emancipator as he lives in the hearts of millions of people. "Simplicity is its predominating characteristic. . . . The tall, ungainly figure embodies in its attitude and in every hanging fold of the unfitted garments, the spirit of infinite tenderness, melancholy and strength."

The Logan and the Sherman monuments are both fine interpretations of the men they represent. General John A. Logan rides with "the air of a conqueror. The body seems a living thing." The statue of the great Civil War general William T. Sherman "is infused with the spirit of invincible determination."

Other notable works of this great sculptor are his "Puritan" and his statue of Philips Brooks, which so well depicts the noble spirit of the man. But his chef d'oeuvre is the Adams memorial in the Rock Creek Cemetery near Washington, D.C. Commissioned by Henry Adams in memory of his wife, the bronze figure conveys a feeling of spiritual exhaustion and reveals "the sense of doubt that is the tragedy of the modern mind."

St. Gaudens was appointed one of the committee to lay out the World's Fair grounds at Chicago, and he personally designed the figure of Christopher Columbus in front of the Administration Building. He was always interested in furthering the cause of American art. He helped largely in founding the American Academy of Fine Arts in Rome, and in developing the artistic beauty of the National Capitol at Washington.

Honors began to press in upon him. Harvard, Yale, and Princeton gave him degrees. At Paris in 1900 he was awarded the medal of honor, and at Buffalo a special medal was given him by his fellow artists who "sought lovingly to exalt him as the master of them all." In 1904 he was elected honorary foreign academician of the Royal Academy of London, and the French government made him an officer of the Legion of Honor and a corresponding member of the Society of Fine Arts. But ever the United States grew more dear to him. "Although of foreign birth and for many years resident abroad, he remained as distinctly American in his art as if he had come from a long line of native ancestors."

Mr. St. Gaudens died on August 3, 1907.

Samuel Gompers

IN 1863 a boy aged thirteen entered the United States as an immigrant from London. His only schooling was obtained in a day school from his sixth to his tenth year, with four years of evening school later. But he was eager to learn, often forgetting to eat in his absorption in his books. This boy grew to be one of the most influential men in the labor movement of his day and was given the title of "Labor Statesman of the World."

Once an object of supercilious contempt, laughed at by capitalists and government officials for his visions of the future status of the working man and for his untiring efforts to secure fair treatment for him, Samuel Gompers, as president of the American Federation of Labor, was the acknowledged leader of nearly three million men organized in labor unions. A few months before his death, the London *Times* devoted an editorial to a eulogy of him, and another influential journal said that "no man in the United States except President Wilson wielded such power as did Mr. Gompers." Here is an illustration of his influence: A former Commissioner of Indian Affairs prepared plans for a series of public improvements on a certain reservation, proposing to use Indian labor at the current hourly wage. As most of the Indians had to come a long distance from home, it was found necessary to substitute a ten-hour day for the legal eight, with only five working days in the week. Some-one called attention to this plan as a violation of the statute limiting hours of work done by government em-ployees. The Commissioner therefore tried to have an amendment passed making the statute nonapplicable to work done by Indians on their own reservations. When he brought his measure before the appropriate Congres-sional Committee he was asked, "Have you seen Gomp-ers?" There appeared to be no alternative, so Gompers was consulted. He promptly vetoed the project which, therefore, had to be abandoned.

After World War I, at a great gathering in Chicago attended by governors of a dozen states, Samuel Gomp-ers received a hearty endorsement in appreciation of the work he had done to unite the labor leaders of Europe in wholehearted support of the Allied war efforts.

It was his quiet determination, his tenacity of purpose, that brought him to the place of honor and influence which he attained. Although born in London in 1850 he was a Hollander by descent. He attributed to his mother, whose parents, he said, were highly educated, his own love of study and his desire to benefit his fellow men.

"Labor organization is the bulwark of democracy" was his theory and practical faith. He began early to work toward its realization. A cigar-maker at fifteen, he helped to organize the first cigar-maker's union of New York. Ten years later he was elected its secretary. He also served as its president for six successive terms. For thirty-six years he worked at his trade, afterwards devoting his time and strength to the betterment of the condition of the working classes.

In 1881 his local union took part in the formation of a national organization. It was a day of small beginnings, for there were but seven delegates, of whom Mr. Gompers was one. He was its president continuously, with the exception of one term. Under his efficiency and personal power its membership rose to nearly three million. At an annual meeting of the American Federation of Labor in 1908 his rule of action, "Partisan to no political party but partisan to a principle," was approved by the organization. He urged upon working people "the imperative necessity and solemn duty of resisting by all means at their command the tendency on the part of the employers and princes of finance to establish in some form or other in this country political and judicial despotism."

When World War I began, his devotion to democracy inspired him with enthusiasm for the cause of the Allies. It was an indication of the force of his personality that he secured from the Federation a pledge of undivided support of the war. At the same time, he demonstrated his skill as a strategist in demanding, as a fundamental prerequisite to cooperation, recognition by the government of employees as a group having common interests; thus maintaining the union principle. The result was a closer relation between Labor and the Federal Administration than had ever existed previously. It has been said that Mr. Gompers was a member of the President's Cabinet in all but the name. He furthered the creation of a Federal Department of Labor, and it became the chief agency of the government for dealing with labor disputes relating to wartime production. Mr. Gompers' office was of great influence in supplying initiative for important decisions. In a speech at Buffalo, New York, President Wilson took occasion to speak of Gompers' "patriotic courage, his large vision, his statesmanlike sense and mind that knew how to pull in harness."

For many years Mr. Gompers endeavored to secure for labor unions exemption from the operation of the Sherman Antitrust Act, a law passed by Congress in 1850 to restrict the size of large corporations, and later expanded, in the Clayton Act, to restrain railroads and unions as well. Gompers was finally successful.

Gompers was not a socialist and it was his constant endeavor to prevent the Federation of Labor from endorsing socialistic policies. He frankly said that he was at variance with the philosophy of socialism and its doctrines. "Economically they are unsound; socially they are wrong; industrially they are an impossibility." He did not approve of force or violence; despite his ardor for the success of the war for democracy, he was a pacifist, a peacemaker. His declaration to the Chicago Federation on strikes was:

> We cannot win by thuggery or violence. Brutality only grows. If we had to win by that method, it would be better to lose. Violence and thuggery only hurt our movement . . . . When compulsion is used, only resentment is aroused and the end is not gained. Only through moral suasion and appeal to men's reason can a movement succeed.

The I.W.W., the Industrial Workers of the World, a revolutionary group of unionists whose goal was the overthrow of capitalism in favor of a socialist society, received no support from him. He did not agree with their theory that one class must be uprooted to give place to another. Give the working men good wages, homes and living conditions, he said, and there would be no occasion to disturb anyone.

The personality of Mr. Gompers is, of course, largely revealed in what has already been said of him, but it is interesting to have a pen picture of him. He was short and heavily built, with massive head and broad shoulders; his hair was long and gray, brushed back severely from his forehead. He wore spectacles over eyes that were keen but kindly.

Deliberation was a prominent characteristic and he was cautious in the extreme. William Hard described him as going out on a new idea as cautiously as an elephant going over a new bridge. He proved himself to be an incorruptible leader and a master strategist. His methods of accomplishing his aims were by preparation, patience, conciliation, and delay. In debate he waited until his opponent had exhausted all his arguments and then adroitly turned back the same arguments. He knew well how to concentrate all his efforts upon a single purpose; it was the secret of his brilliant career. He allowed nothing to divert his mind from his one aim of helping the working man to better his condition. "Gompersian forcefulness" is the name given by one writer to his way of steadily pushing forward to his goal. An Englishman says: "The most persistent journalist could not sidetrack him where he did not want to go. He quietly, so to speak, shunted himself back onto the main line, pushing the journalist before him."

For a man who had little schooling, it is remarkable that he acquired such correct use of the English language. He was thoroughly familiar with the best literature in three languages besides English, and he had unusual ability in writing pamphlets. He lectured at Harvard, Cornell, Michigan, and Wisconsin universities.

Although finally receiving a yearly salary of $7,000, as president of the Federation of Labor, Mr. Gompers was by no means even a well-to-do man. He gave so largely to union men who were in need that his own family were sometimes decidedly limited in their expenditures. For the first four years of his presidency he received nothing; for the next five, he had $1,200 a year. Aware of his poverty, Governor Hill of New York offered him the post of Commissioner of Arbitration at a salary of $3,000 a year; yet, though he was earning scarcely twenty dollars a week at the time, he refused the offer. Other advantageous positions were suggested to him, among them a nomination to Congress and a place on the Industrial Commission, but one and all were declined, a striking evidence of his steadfast adherence to his life purpose. The records of a manufacturing association gave proof that he was also offered $4,500 in cash and a sinecure for life, which was likewise refused. Is it any wonder that he was devotedly loved by thousands of American working men?

Mr. Gompers was active to the last. While on a visit to Mexico City, in the cause of labor, he was suddenly stricken. A special train rushed him to the border, but he grew worse and died in San Antonio, Texas, on December 13, 1924. He was seventy-four years old. Tributes from all political parties and from all over the world testified to the high esteem in which he was held.

Felix Adler

" A PERSONALITY of spiritual majesty and light; one
does him unconscious reverence." This is a tribute
that not one person only, but many would give to Dr.
Adler after his fifty years of devotion to a great cause—
the cause of moral righteousness.

When as a young man Felix Adler broke away from
the Jewish faith to begin a noble lifework in accordance
with his intellectual belief and moral insight, there must
have been a strange wrench to himself, to his family,
and to the large body of synagogue members who knew
him as the able son of his revered father. Brought up in
the traditions and faith of an orthodox Jewish home,
with his father a devout and scholarly German Rabbi,
who had become leader of the great Temple Emanu El
of New York City, Felix had been destined for the Jewish rabbinate.

He was born in Alzey, Germany, in 1851, and for
twenty years of his life German as well as Jewish influences were around him. He attended Columbia University and then went to study at Berlin and Heidelberg,
obtaining his Ph.D. in 1873. He returned to America

but not to follow in his father's footsteps. Many influences affected his clear thinking and earnest spirit. He had known Ralph Waldo Emerson at home and studied Immanuel Kant abroad. It was a time when biblical criticism and the principle of evolution were bringing light to many minds. Adler's conception of life and truth and his passion for sincerity could not allow him to hold to rituals, ceremonies, and many Mosaic Laws, or to a God of a chosen and superior people. He believed all races were equal and interdependent; he had faith in the high worth of every human being.

For two years he served as Professor of Hebrew and Oriental Literature at Cornell University. In 1876 Dr. Adler returned to New York City and established the Society for Ethical Culture amid considerable controversy. It was first organized under the name of "Union for the Higher Life," among a group of young men friends, and was based on three tacit assumptions: sexpurity; the principle of devoting the surplus of one's income beyond that required for one's own genuine needs to the elevation of the working class; and, thirdly, continued intellectual development.

The society grew in numbers and power with many prominent Jews becoming members. However, Dr. Adler's ideal had been nonsectarian, interracial, and interreligious, positing ethics as the basis of all religions, and many of the members of the society have been non-Jewish. In the society theology has no place, and the differences of Judaism and Christianity are set aside. There is no formal creed. It dedicates itself simply to "promoting the knowledge, the love, and the practice of the right." The words over the New York Meeting House are these: "The place where men seek the Highest is holy ground."

No man could be more reverent or less partisan in spirit than was Felix Adler. A story is told of his being in a group of ministers one day, and a conversation was started on what question each would ask if Jesus came into the room. After several questions had been suggested, Dr. Adler was asked what he would say. His reply was, "I should be silent, lost in wonder and awe." (In his writings he refers to Jesus as the highest of the Hebrew prophets.)

Through many years he gave discourses on Sunday morning to the Society of Ethical Culture. Dr. Henry Neumann, in speaking of the Ethical Movement, said it had been religious from the beginning. He quoted from Emerson, "The progress of religion is steadily to its identity with morals," and added, "Rationalistic objections to dogmas were not the chief occasion why Felix Adler went out from the faith of his fathers. The leading impulse was the need of a new consecrating influence."

This "consecrating influence" developed into a moral enthusiasm. The right for the right's sake was its basis. It would be an injustice to attempt to outline Dr. Adler's *Ethical Philosophy of Life* in this brief sketch—his various writings and especially his book under this title must give that insight. An extract or two may reveal something of his character and thought; he insisted that life must be one of constant advance.

> The supremacy of the moral end of life above all other ends, the sufficiency of man for the pursuit of that end, the increase of moral truth to be expected from loyalty in this pursuit—these are the three tenets, if we may call them so, of an ethical creed . . . . By ceaseless efforts to live the good life we maintain our moral sanity. Not from without, but from within, flow the divine waters that renew the soul. The ethical element of religion has ever been its truly vital and quickening force. It is this which lends such majesty to the speeches of the Prophets, which gives such ineffable power and sweetness to the words of Jesus. Has this ethical element become less important in our age? Has the need of accentuating it become less imperative? Today, in the estimation of many, science and art are taking the place of religion. But science and art alike are inadequate to build up character and to furnish binding rules of conduct . . . .
>
> Let us produce, through the efficacy of a better moral life and of a deeper moral experience, a surer faith in the ultimate victory of the good.

In discussing "The Moral Ideal," Dr. Adler said:

> The moral ideal should be conceived as a supreme society rather than as a supreme individual . . . . The creative endeavor to realize, or approximate to the realization of

the infinite organic scheme, in terms of actual social progress replaces worship in the older sense as homage toward a single being regarded as embodying in himself the totality of moral excellence. Union with the infinite is the experience within oneself of the compelling impulse that issues from the idea of infinite organism, and the sense that the worth of life consists, despite the tragic shortcomings, in unremitting effort to yield obedience to the impulse.

Societies for Ethical Culture have not spread to a great many cities, and their membership has not grown to large numbers. This is probably due to the fact that there is a cold intellectual quality, one might almost say a hardness, about their belief and their services. While their author had a passion for righteousness, it was so restrained by a calm philosophy that there is little emotional contagion.

The Ethical Culture School established by the New York Society for Ethical Culture began as a kindergarten in 1878—the first free kindergarten to be opened in New York City. The school soon grew to over nine hundred pupils and later expanded even further. Eventually it included a normal school and a pre-vocational Art High School besides other high schools.

A number of pioneer social enterprises must be credited to the New York Society for Ethical Culture: the free kindergarten, when this means of education was little appreciated or even known by many persons; manual training for the elementary school grades; district nursing when it was introduced into this country; festivals and dramatic presentations which later led to civic festivals; organization of classes for adult education.

Felix Adler said:

> If education is to improve mankind, the first imperative necessity is that education itself be improved . . . . To improve human conditions it is necessary to improve human beings. The converse also is true: better people to achieve better conditions, better conditions to have better people —the effort of change must be undertaken from both ends.

In the announcement of the Ethical Culture Preprofessional School, he emphasized:

> Any plan for the creation of a better world to live in, as peace instead of war, the spirit of coöperation between employers and workers, and more of beauty and enduring felicity in sex relations, is not feasible unless individual men and women are educated to meet the requirements of the plan.

Felix Adler labored with Theodore Roosevelt, Jacob Riis, and others for tenement reform and municipal welfare in New York City. He gave himself to the cause of rescuing children from child labor. For seventeen years and up to 1921, he was chairman of the National Child Labor Committee, which, as he said, "seeks to put an end to the national disgrace of child mistreatment and at the same time to promote every enterprise that looks to-

ward a wiser and more efficient education of our youth."
This organization took thousands of children out of the
mills and in later years turned its special attention to securing freedom and better conditions for children who
labored on farms. Dr. Adler said:

> [In considering] what it is at bottom that accounts for
> so monstrous a thing as the use of child labor, especially
> among a people like ours—so quick to resent oppression,
> so readily sympathetic with suffering—I have come to the
> conclusion that here we come upon the seamy side of our
> evaluation of efficiency. We are keen to bring things to
> pass, we put our very selves into work and so we come to
> estimate the human factor, not in terms of what a man is,
> but of what he produces, and we come to think of a little
> child, not as it is, a germ of spiritual life as yet not un-
> folded, a precious asset for the future of the world, but we
> are prone to think of the child in terms of what even
> these little hands, this weary little body can be coerced to
> produce. The movement against Child Labor, therefore,
> has had for me a great significance of making an inroad
> in this country on the habit of sacrificing personality to
> the work; if we can make people respect the really human
> factor in the child, they will be more prepared to respect
> the same in the adult.

Dr. Adler's interpretation of a citizen is "one who
helps to realize the purpose for which this nation exists."
For many years he was professor of Political and Social
Ethics at Columbia University. He was exchange professor at the University of Berlin in 1908–09, and Hibbert

lecturer at Oxford in May 1923. He was president of the Eastern Division of the American Philosophical Association in 1928.

In his many writings he set forth with great clarity his ethical and philosophical conceptions at the time they were written: *Creed and Deed* in 1877, *Ethics of the Political Situation* in 1884. Helpful counsel is given in Dr. Adler's *Moral Instruction of Children* (1902), and his high conception of marriage is shown in *Marriage and Divorce* (1905). His *Religion of Duty* and *Essentials of Spirituality* were written about this time; *The World Crisis and Its Meaning* in 1915; and *An Ethical Philosophy of Life* a few years later. *Life and Destiny* is a collection of extracts from Dr. Adler's lectures and is full of helpful suggestions; *The Reconstruction of the Spiritual Ideal* (1923) is the crown of his ideas.

He was the chief editor of *The Standard,* the organ of the American Ethical Union, "to promote ethical thinking and to encourage better ways of living."

Dr. Adler's contribution to the world was one of high spiritual appeal. His moral ideal was so exalted that he was, inevitably, discouraged by the disparity between that ideal and the real world in which he worked. At the end of his career he said:

> I look back on my life and its net results. I have seen spiritual ideals and the more clearly I see them, the wider appears the distance between them and the empirical conditions, the changes I could effect in those conditions. I

have worked in social reform, and the impression I have been able to make now seems to me so utterly insignificant as to make my early sanguine aspirations appear pathetic . . . . I look lastly into my heart, my own character, and the effort I have made to fuse the discordant elements to achieve a genuine integrity there, and I find the disappointment there the deepest of all.

Yet, it has been said that Dr. Adler's real greatness did not lie in any of the things that he did, but in the man himself, in his *being*. Though he died on April 24, 1933, the influence of his powerful personality remains, like that of the great prophets, as a symbol of man's aspiration for moral righteousness.

Ottmar Mergenthaler

I N these days of the multiplicity of the printed page
we may well remember the man who invented the
Linotype, which enables an operator to set type much
faster than it can be done by hand. The inventor of this
machine came to the United States from Germany in
1872. He was born in May 1854, at Bietigheim, located
some twenty miles from Stuttgart. His father was a
teacher, his mother also belonged to a family which for
many years had practiced that profession. The boy was
educated at his father's school. At home he was not allowed much time for play, for he had to help cook the
meals, wash dishes, build fires during the winter, and
take care of the garden in the summer. The year round
he was expected to feed the pigs and cattle.

At the age of fourteen Ottmar was supposed to begin
his training as a teacher, but he was not interested in the
profession. He had a special liking for mechanics, having kept clocks in repair and made models of animals
out of wood. He chose to become an apprentice to Mr.
Hahl, his stepmother's brother who made watches and
clocks. The terms were four years' service without

wages. He was also to pay a small premium and provide his own tools. Board and lodging were to be furnished by his employer. Ottmar had a pleasant home with Mr. Hahl, and he enjoyed his work as well as the company of the other young workers. He developed unusual skill and mechanical talent and succeeded so well that wages were paid him a year before the expiration of his apprenticeship. The rarity of the young man's ability is evident from the fact that this was the first time in a business life of over thirty years that Mr. Hahl had found occasion so to recognize talent in any youth.

In the evening Ottmar took lessons in mechanical drawing, which later proved to be of much advantage to him in the drafting of his inventions. In 1872 at the close of his four years' apprenticeship, he had to decide where to locate for starting a business of his own. The close of the Franco-Prussian War had left conditions in Germany very unsatisfactory. There was a large amount of unemployment, and increased military duties were causing many young men to leave the country. Ottmar therefore decided to do likewise, and applied to August Hahl, son of his late employer and a maker of electrical instruments in Washington, D.C., for a loan of passage money to be repaid by working in his factory. The money was promptly sent, and Mergenthaler landed in Baltimore in October 1872, going at once to Washington.

Electrical instruments were unfamiliar to him, but he

soon mastered their workings, and within two years he was made foreman of the shop, even acting as business manager when Mr. Hahl was absent. The United States Signal Service had been established only a short time earlier, and Mergenthaler's work consisted largely of making the standard instruments for the Service. For this he appeared to have special fitness.

Washington was a place where inventor's models, which were required whenever anyone filed an application for a patent, were particularly built, and this brought Mergenthaler into contact with many inventors and stimulated his own talent in that direction. In August 1876, his attention was attracted to the model of a writing machine. He examined it and saw how to remedy its defects. He was commissioned to build a machine of full-size, and he did so in 1877. But though much improved, it never would be a real success.

In January 1883, several of his Washington friends asked Mergenthaler to try to devise a machine to take the place of typesetting done by hand, which was a slow and laborious process. On New Year's Day he dissolved the partnership with Mr. Hahl, which had existed for two years, and started in business for himself. Settling in Baltimore he proceeded to work out the desires of his friends.

He worked unsuccessfully for several years and then came up with the idea of using a single bar of metal to carry a composed line of type. His machine would hold matrices—narrow bars of metal with the letters of the alphabet and other characters incised on them, cut into them. As the operator pressed the keys of the machine, the matrices would drop down into a channel. When a single line of type was composed, fluid metal would pour over it. A finished line of type, shining like silver, would drop from the machine while each matrix would be sent back to its receptacle. All this was done within fifty seconds. It was a notable event in the history of printing.

His backers needed persuasion before they were willing to endorse the new idea, but finally they gave the order to Mergenthaler to build two machines according to his plan. In 1884 when the first of these machines was ready to be tested a dozen spectators came to see the operation. Everything went off well.

During the next two years the inventor improved and simplified his Linotype. In February 1855, he exhibited a much improved machine at the Chamberlain Hotel in Washington. Printers from all over the world were interested. A banquet followed in honor of the inventor's great achievement. But still later Mergenthaler saw that to make the machine more perfect he would have to construct it so that the operator could watch its motions and what he was doing. Whitelaw Reid, editor of the New York *Tribune,* gave the Linotype its name. He was the first to use the new invention in printing his newspaper. At the close of 1886 a dozen of the machines were at work in the *Tribune* offices. The Chicago *Inter-Ocean* and the Louisville *Courier-Journal* also adopted it. In 1880 big profits were gained from the Linotype. The New York *Tribune* saved $80,000 within twelve months. And yet the inventor's royalty was only fifty dollars per machine.

Still Mergenthaler continued to make improvements until he had at last a wonderfully perfect machine. As it now stands, its method of working, briefly told, is as follows: The operator has before him the control of about 1,500 matrices. Each matrix, or mold, is a small flat plate of brass that has on its outer edge an incised letter, and its upper end a series of teeth for distributing purposes. As the operator touches a key the desired letter is set free and glides in full view to its assembling place. In like manner each letter reaches its destination until the word is completed. Then the operator touches a key that inserts a space shaped like a double wedge. When the line of type is full, it is justified by moving a lever, and it is carried automatically to a mold where liquid metal is forced against the matrices and spaces. Then the line of type is ready to be printed. This slug, as it is called, in a moment is hard and cool enough to pass to a tray where other slugs are swiftly added to form a page or column ready for the printing press. A set of matrices often replaces a font of type weighing two hundred times as much. A section of the machine returns the matrices to their boxes as quickly as 270 a minute and unerringly, unless a matrix is bent by accident or otherwise injured. In a Linotype three distinct operations go on together: composing one line, casting a second, and distributing a third, so that the machine has a pace exceeding that at which an expert operator can finger his keys.

Mergenthaler was beloved by all the men who worked for him. He was good to all of them and, no matter how humble their station, he always had a kind word for them and a friendly word to say of them.

Worn out from hard work, he contracted tuberculosis in 1894, and five years later he died, but not before he received awards in recognition of his great ability: a medal from the Cooper Institute of New York; the John Scott medal from the City of Philadelphia; and the Elliott Cresson gold medal from the Franklin Institute of Philadelphia.

Charles Proteus Steinmetz

A GREAT mind in a small body—he stood only four feet high and carried an enormous head between high shoulders—one of the world's greatest mathematicians, a mental dynamo. So was Charles Proteus Steinmetz described when he was professor of electrical engineering in Union College, Schenectady, N.Y., and the highly valued consulting engineer of the General Electric Company of the same city. Distinguished as he became, he belonged to a poor family in Breslau, Germany, where he was born on April 9, 1865. His father, a lithographer by trade but later a railroad employee, was determined that his son should be well educated and did everything in his power toward that end. In order to test fully his tastes and capabilities Charles took preparatory courses in medicine, political economy, mechanical engineering, and other studies in the University of Breslau. Finally he gave himself to full and comprehensive work in mathematics, higher chemistry, and electricity.

During his student days Steinmetz was arrested by the repressive German government for membership in a socialist club. Later he was released, but a fellow student was remanded for trial. Steinmetz obtained permission to bring his friend writing materials so that he might finish his doctor's thesis while in jail. He was also allowed to bring toilet articles, such as toothpaste. And his friend was permitted to have books, though each book that Steinmetz brought to the jail was rigorously inspected by a government agent before it was allowed in the prisoner's cell. After the trial at which this medical student was acquitted, the prosecuting agent was dismayed to discover that he had passed on to the prisoner books whose blank pages were covered with invisible writing. The student had been able to develop the writing with a solution made from the toothpaste and blotting paper. From suggestions thus made to him, he had been able to work out his defense. Steinmetz, who had made the invisible ink and had planned the whole affair, found the country an unsafe place to stay in and escaped to Switzerland in 1888. A year later he emigrated to the United States.

Here he worked for a time at twelve dollars a week with Eickemeyer and Company in Yonkers, New York. While there his loneliness as a stranger in a strange land was relieved one evening by an acquaintance who invited him to his home for supper. In grateful recognition of this act of friendliness he later adopted a son of the poor family, and it is believed that he assisted in the education of others.

In 1894 after the General Electric Company had consolidated the Eickemeyer business with its own, the headquarters were transferred to Schenectady. Soon afterward Steinmetz became its consulting engineer at a salary which stood for some time at $100,000 a year. In 1902 he also accepted the professorship of electrical engineering at Union College. The clarity of his exposition of even the most intricate problems made his lectures stimulating and rewarding. Consequently the college was considered one of the best for the study of electrical engineering.

Dr. Steinmetz was a scientist with a passion for work, uniting the imagination of an artist with a force and intensity that compelled him to make a thorough search into all that was involved in any subject that presented itself to him for observation. Having acquired a command of the English language and the ability to make difficult things easy to understand, he was noted not only as a lecturer but also as a writer for magazines. At meetings of the American Institute of Electrical Engineers, of which he was for some years president, he was usually called upon to close the discussions because of his power of lucid description and explanation, given in forceful and clean-cut phrases.

What did this remarkable man do to benefit in a practical way all the people of America?

For many years engineers had been concerned with regulating the electric energy derived from rivers and waterfalls. After a profound study of the problem Dr.

Steinmetz devised a method by which these forces could be restrained so that today it is possible to transmit electrical power at high pressure without damage. This is technically called high voltage for power transmission, and it is not unusual now for 200,000 volts to be safely used.

He showed us the possibility of abandoning generating plants of small capacity and furnishing electrical power by substation service from the big trunk supply lines.

He greatly benefited all industry by his invention of various motors, such as the induction and polyphase motors. These made possible quick elevator service and better street lighting. The Steinmetz Law of Magnetism is a method by which engineers can figure how much magnetizing current they should use to magnetize a given piece of iron to be used in an electrical generator or motor, and how hot the iron will become when used in certain conditions. This is considered one of the most valuable things he did.

Dr. Steinmetz was a man of remarkable humility despite his wonderful scientific ability. He invented many other things in addition to the motors mentioned above, particularly a magnetite arc lamp and a mercury arc rectifier. But it was a notable characteristic of his that he was continually giving suggestions to others, helping them to perfect their own inventions. He was so highly regarded, not only by members of his own profession but also by his townsmen, that he held for some years the office of President of the Board of Education of Schenectady and later was made President of the Common Council of that city.

He was very much interested in the National Association of Corporation Schools, of which he became president. The object of this organization was to correlate the educational opportunities of all engaged in industrial work, so that illiteracy and inefficiency might be lessened and production speeded up, and thereby compensation and the standard of living might be raised. He was a socialist of the kind indicated by the following words of his:

"We must let the big corporations alone . . . [there is] no use in breaking them up into smaller units which cannot be controlled. As soon as the big ones combine under stricter government regulations, the sooner we shall have better working conditions."

The benefits conferred by him upon America may well have caused Germany to regret that she compelled him to leave his native land.

At his death, which occurred suddenly October 26, 1923, when he was only fifty-eight years of age, appreciation was shown in several ways by the people of the United States. In his home city the public schools were closed the day he died, and flags were at half-mast while his body lay in state. In newspapers and other periodicals his achievements were discussed, and noted scientists paid tribute to "the little cripple with a giant mind." Dr. Steinmetz had proved himself not only a great electrician but a great mathematician. He was an exponent of pure science and applied science also. His service to electrical science was incalculable. From a popular standpoint, his invention of artificial lightning and an "indoor thunderstorm" were of greatest interest. The simplicity of his writings caused some of them to find place in general as well as scientific magazines, and his "Electricity and Civilization" and "Science and Religion" appeared in *Harper's Magazine* the year before his death. Like many men, he believed that science and religion were not incompatible.

Hideyo Noguchi

IN the northern Aizu district of Honshu, the main island of Japan, stands the magnificent volcanic cone of Bandai. It is inactive now except for a plume of smoke that sometimes leaps from it to stain the blue sky. But twelve hundred years ago it was in eruption, the lava from it destroying whole villages and damming a mountain stream. The backed-up stream formed a beautiful lake, and on its shores, in the shadow of the great mountain, stands the little agricultural village of Okinajima.

Its inhabitants were poor in 1868, for the Japanese revolution which had overthrown the feudal shoguns, or war lords, had just been concluded. Aizu, a mountain stronghold of feudalism, had held out to the last, and it had been occupied, at great cost, by the soldiers of the Emperor.

Shika Noguchi, whose father was the poorest of the inhabitants of Okinajima, long remembered the occupation, for she and her sickly father had been put out of their house by the soldiers. But Shika remembered something else. She remembered that five generations ago, in the time of Seitaro Noguchi, the house of Noguchi had been a distinguished one. And she prayed to the gods for its restoration. Though she was a poor farm girl in service as a maid in the house of the priest Uno Ura, she accepted his offer to teach her to write. They saved the cost of ink and paper for practicing by sprinkling ashes on a lacquered tray and shaping the ideographs in the ash. The girl learned quickly, and she remembered what she learned, thinking perhaps of her famous ancestors and of the way in which her new-found knowledge might help her to restore her family's dignity.

There was, however, a strong possibility that the Noguchi family would soon be extinct. Shika was the last of the line and, lacking a dowry, she had little hope of winning a husband. But in addition to being a girl with a knowledge of writing, she was strong and a most excellent farmer, far more important considerations in an agricultural community where the women work as hard as the men, standing in the muddy waters of the rice fields from dawn to dusk in winter and in summer. One day Sayosuke the farmer asked her to marry him. Shika agreed, taking the precaution to adopt her future husband first, as is the custom in Japan when one is the last of one's house. Her children would thus bear the Noguchi name. And they would be their mother's children in more than name and birth, for Sayosuke was fond of drinking saki and didn't care for responsibility. When Inu, a girl child, was born, he was disappointed.

And when the second child was born, on November 24, 1876, though it was a boy and an occasion for gladness, Shika's husband left her and the two children in the little one-room hut, the only possession which had not yet been sold for saki. Sayosuke went off to live on another island, leaving Shika to care for the children as best she could, only coming back from time to time to beg money from the hard-working girl.

Shika called her son Seisaku, a name which, in conformity with Japanese custom, he would exchange upon reaching maturity, becoming Hideyo Noguchi. "Greatman-of-the-world" is a rough translation of his chosen name, an appellation surely prophetic of his later career. But at the time we are speaking of there was no hint of that great future. Indeed, his mother was so poor that she could not afford to pay anyone a few yen to watch him for her during the day. She had to carry him into the fields with her, depositing him upon a bank while she worked among the rice plants. Later, when his sister Inu was a little older, she left the boy with her. He would sleep close beside the urori, a brazier used for cooking, which provided the only warmth in the little hut. When he awoke, his sister would try to keep the active little three year old out of mischief.

One day, however, Shika was longer than usual in the rice fields. It began to get dark, and Inu, frightened, went to look for her mother. As she walked through the darkening fields, a high-pitched scream from the house she had just left shattered the quietness of the evening. It was followed by another. And another. Turning toward the noise, she saw her mother flash by, tearing savagely at the heavy warazi, the thick clogs to which the sticky mud of the fields clung. Barefoot, Shika raced into the house and snatched her son from the urori, where he was scrambling among the hot coals. Neighbors rushed in.

There was no doctor in the small village, but one of the men examined the boy. "The fingers of the left hand are mostly gone," he said, "and the left arm and the left foot and the right hand are burned, I know not how badly."

The days that followed were terrible ones for Shika. Infection set in, and the little boy almost died. For twenty-one days Shika did not leave her son night or day. She kept her sleepless eyes open by wedging bits of wood between the lids. And as she nursed the boy back to health, she gradually straightened the crumpled fingers of the right hand, manipulating them until they gained strength. For the left hand she could do nothing. It remained a crooked stump with a few knoblike protrusions where the fingers had been.

Gradually Seisaku recovered. Hereafter, his mother would take him with her wherever she went, hanging the basket in which he slept in a tree while she worked, or letting him romp in the fields nearby where she could watch him. As he grew, Shika kept him close to her, teaching him what she had learned in the household of the priest. By the time he was ready for school, he was already far in advance of his classmates. Jealous of his learning, they began to taunt him, shouting "Tembo, tembo," or "hand boy," in mockery of his deformed hand. Angered by their taunts, the boy withdrew to his books, studying harder when he realized that he could never become a good farmer with his misshapen hand.

However, the cost of attending school was a severe drain, and young Seisaku had to work to keep himself there. Mornings he would fish in Lake Inawashiro, selling his catch in the town before going to class. After school he carried baggage, often traveling as far as ten miles with a heavy burden through winter snows. At night he tended the wood fire that heated the water in the communal bath house. He got no money for this latter job, but he was allowed to read in the light of the fire. At home he could not read after the sun went down because it was always dark there, the family being too poor to buy fuel for such purposes.

Through the assistance of Sakae Kobayashi, a kindly school principal from Inawashiro who recognized his ability, Seisaku was able to enter the kotto-shogakko, the Japanese secondary school. There he soon excelled even his teachers in such subjects as drawing, science, and English, and he was at the head of the class in all of his subjects. Finishing his own work rapidly, he would help his fellow students with theirs. He would help, that is, if they pretended to ignore his deformed left hand, which he was extremely sensitive about and tried to conceal, drawing it up into the wide sleeve of his kimono. But Kobayashi-san had seen the useless hand and he thought that something might be done for it by a skillful doctor. Taking up a collection among the fathers of the boys in the kotto-shogakko, he sent young Seisaku off to Waka-matsu one wonderful day with money to see a doctor he had heard of in that city.

Seisaku walked the twenty miles to Wakamatsu with rising hope in his heart. There he saw the strange doctor who had been educated abroad and who wore trousers and a waistcoat instead of the traditional kimono. Kanae Watanabe was his name, and after examining the boy's hand carefully, he told him that much could be done for it. He wished to operate immediately. Would Seisaku like something to deaden the pain? The boy shook his head. "But if you have a book, let me read it mean-while," he said.

Many treatments followed the initial operation, Seisaku walking the twenty miles to be treated and twenty miles back home. But Watanabe-san was a great doctor, and he worked miracles with the hand. He could not, of course, restore the fingers. But he separated the stumps, enabling each to move independently and perform useful functions. And the scar tissue that had drawn the hand to the wrist was severed, allowing the hand to hang naturally. Seisaku had, in effect, a new hand. And he had a new aim as well. He was determined to be a doctor.

Talking with the doctor while he was being treated, Seisaku gave voice to his ambition. Since the doctor needed another boy in his house to run errands, mix medicines, and help with patients, Seisaku was apprenticed to him at once. He would learn what he could through observation. He would also have access to the doctor's library, which included many works in English, German, and French, as well as medical texts in Japanese. Seisaku knew no German or French, but he soon took advantage of the opportunities of this relatively large city to find someone who would teach him those languages. And so that he might have more time for studying, he cut his sleeping time down to three hours a night, imitating Napoleon, whom he read about in one of Dr. Watanabe's books.

With the outbreak of the first Sino-Japanese war Dr. Watanabe, an ex-military surgeon, left for the front, leaving young Seisaku in charge of his domestic affairs. When he returned in 1894, he was delighted to find his household account books in perfect order and his affairs running smoothly. He was overwhelmed when he discovered that the boy, studying by himself, had quite prepared himself for the first examinations at the Tokyo Medical School. The passing of these examinations admitted him to the school with advanced standing, and he entered the institution later that year with financial help from Dr. Watanabe and his old friend and teacher Kobayashi-san.

In Tokyo Seisaku lived on next to nothing. Dr. Chiwaki, a friend whom he had met at Dr. Watanabe's home, worked in the Takagama Dental College there, and he got Seisaku a job ringing the class bell and polishing the school lamps. When Seisaku lost his job because he became interested in a book and forgot to ring the bell signifying the end of class, Dr. Chiwaki contributed fifteen yen a month to the boy's support. In this way Seisaku continued at the Medical College. A poor one by modern standards and frowned upon even in those days by graduates of the Imperial University, the college offered little beyond a rather uninspired series of lectures. But Seisaku stuck it out for three years, graduating in 1897. Passing the government examination, he became a licensed physician and surgeon.

Hideyo, as young Noguchi began to call himself about this time, did not go into practice as a physician upon being licensed. Ever since the day he had first looked through a microscope in the house of Dr. Watanabe, he had wanted to be a bacteriologist and study the minute organisms that he had observed beneath the lens. But before he could undertake independent research, much more study would be necessary. He would have to go abroad, to America and to Germany, where the great men of science had their laboratories. Meanwhile, he worked at the Jutendo General Hospital, editing a medical journal. Also, through the aid of Dr. Chiwaki, he became a lecturer in general pathology and oral surgery at the Tokyo Dental College. Soon, however, he had an opportunity to follow his inclination for research work, and he joined the staff of Dr. Kitasato at the Government Institute of Infectious Diseases. He was even promised that he would be able to study abroad under government sponsorship. But he would have to wait five years for that.

In the meantime, bubonic plague had broken out in China, and Noguchi was sent to New Chwang under the auspices of the International Sanitary Board. He was made physician-in-chief to the Central Medical Bureau, comprising both a hospital and a bacteriological laboratory. Later, the plague having disappeared from the region, he was transferred to Manchuria under a Russian medical commission, where he remained until the Boxer Rebellion. Then he returned to Tokyo, busying himself with the publication of several books, including texts on the methods of pathological and bacteriological study and the translation of a German manual of hygiene.

One day while Noguchi was at work at the institute, several American scientists came to visit Dr. Kitasato, who enjoyed an international reputation for his work on diphtheria immunization. Among them was Dr. Simon Flexner, who was returning to America and a new job at the University of Pennsylvania. Noguchi talked with the man, expressing his desire to visit America for study.

Despite the fact that, according to Dr. Flexner, "no particular encouragement was given to this request," Noguchi appeared on the University of Pennsylvania campus the following year, having borrowed 300 yen from his friend Chiwaki to make the trip. He had little money left when he arrived, and there was, of course, no job at the university for the unexpected visitor. But Dr. Flexner did his best for the young Oriental, introducing him to Dr. Silas Weir Mitchell. A man already famous for his work on snake venoms, Dr. Mitchell interested Noguchi in the subject, providing him with funds sufficient to cover the cost of his experiments and a modest sum for living expenses. Noguchi was soon writing confidently to friends in Japan, "I have entered the sweet realm of science."

Having less that $25 a month during his first year in America, Noguchi lived precariously. But his work on the venoms progressed rapidly and, as he expressed it, "except for eating and drinking there is only experimentation." Soon his work was being recognized as important in scientific circles. Dr. Mitchell interested the National Academy of Science in it, and a contribution from the Bache Fund was made to extend the scope of investigation. Later the Carnegie Institute granted funds to the young Japanese scientist. As various aspects of the study were completed, Noguchi published the results in the University of Pennsylvania Medical Bulletin and in other scientific periodicals. Eventually the results of the studies as a whole were brought together in a handsome, illustrated volume published by the Carnegie Institute. But before that happened, Noguchi was given his long-hoped-for opportunity to study in Europe. Receiving a Carnegie fellowship for a year's study abroad, he went to Copenhagen, Denmark, to work under Thorwald Madsen at the Staatens Serum Institute. And when he returned to America, in 1904, a position was awaiting him in the newly opened Rockefeller Institute for Medical Research in New York. Writing home at the beginning of his fifth year away from Japan, Noguchi said, "In fact I will stay in America for a long time. The reason is that it has much more future at every point than Japan."

At the Rockefeller Institute Noguchi worked on a number of problems. He worked on trachoma, a serious eye disease, but temporarily turned from "this rather resultless subject." He published some further observations on venom—the list of his articles had grown to twenty by now. He investigated tetanus. Then he turned to the problem of blood serum. Next he tackled the dread disease syphilis, developing a modification of the famed Wassermann test, and discovering a method of diagnosing *tabes dorsalis,* a form of paralysis caused by the disease, by tapping the spinal fluid. His book on the diagnosis of syphilis followed.

Then, in October of 1910, Noguchi brought one of his most significant pieces of work at the Institute to a triumphant conclusion and thus attracted worldwide attention. That scientific feat was the cultivation of the Spirochaeta pallida, the pale spirochete assumed to be the cause of syphilis. The organism had first been seen by Schaudinn in 1905, but no one had been able to cultivate it by itself, to grow it unmixed with other organisms in what is called a pure culture. Until someone produced the disease in an animal with a pure culture, it could not be determined whether some other organism —unknown, unseen, perhaps unseeable—was not the true cause of the disease. Noguchi solved the riddle by producing the pale spirochete for the first time and infecting a laboratory animal from his culture. From the culture he also developed a product called luetin, of use in detecting latent and congenital syphilis.

Valuable as the specific discovery was, its significance was small compared with the consequence issuing from it, namely, the perfection of a method for the pure cultivation of the class of spirochetal microorganisms. Noguchi now cultivated a horde of spirochetes that no one had been able to cultivate before, including among many others the spirochetes of European and African relapsing fevers. Mastering the field of spirochetes, he turned to other fields, isolating the granular bodies causing trachoma, an eye disease which he had once studied and given up as "resultless."

Then he turned to a still different problem—and a big one. Working on a hunch that general paralysis of the insane is syphilis of the brain, he sought the spirochete of syphilis in the brains of dead paretics, perfecting new microscopic methods of examining the diseased tissue. And he found what he was seeking both in the brain tissues of those who had died of general paralysis and in the spinal cords of victims of locomotor ataxia, thereby linking those two common and terrible diseases and establishing their cause.

Hideyo Noguchi was by now universally recognized as a great man of the world of science. The University of Pennsylvania granted him an honorary degree. He was made a full member of the Rockefeller Institute, along with Dr. Carrel, Professor Loeb, and his former teacher, Dr. Flexner. Offered the presidency of the Peru Research Institute and the directorship of the Agriculture Department of Great Britain, he declined these offers and the large salaries that went with them, preferring to remain in America. His wife, the former Mary Dardis, was an American, and, though prejudicial naturalization laws prevented him from becoming an American citizen, he had adopted her country since his marriage in 1912. He did, however, accept the invitation to lecture before the Versammlung deutscher Naturforscher und Aertze in Vienna. To lecture before those Germans whom he had always considered the great men of science! And when he went abroad, his trip through Europe was a triumphal one. He was recognized and deferred to everywhere. And he was similarly acclaimed on his trip to Japan in 1915, where he was awarded the Imperial Prize of the Japanese Academy.

But fame, that last infirmity of noble minds, was no longer a spur to him. He had long ago asserted his independence of its promptings in a letter written, in his curiously poetic English, to a friend in Japan:

> Since I came to this country I have learned besides science something of the ends of life, something about withering and blooming, what they mean . . . . In this whirlpool of confusion we should keep hope and virtue. If you realize these two it will be happiness. I have already realized one half of my purpose in coming to America and the other half is fate and work. If I confess my ideal when I came it was narrow and small. It was largely, no, it was entirely to get glory. That was first with me. But this thinking has been destroyed and now I want to consecrate my life to one great task.

His life had become completely consecrated to scientific research. After his lecture tours he was eager to get back to his work, for his mind had lain fallow long enough. He returned to America to investigate the fatal Rocky Mountain spotted fever, discovering a serum that would suppress the infection. He settled the question of the relationship between two obscure South American diseases, oroya fever and *verruga peruana*, establishing them as variants of carrion's disease and forwarding work on its carriers. He cultivated the "globoid bodies" from the virus disease poliomyelitis, advancing research in that field. And from 1918, when he became a member of the Rockefeller Foundation Commission sent to Ecuador, until his death in 1928, he worked intermittently on yellow fever. Indeed, it was of that disease that he died in South Africa, like Adrian Stokes, whose conclusions about the disease his own investigations supported. And those conclusions were destructive of his own widely accepted earlier hypothesis about the cause of the disease!

Leading a dedicated life, Hideyo Noguchi was something more than a great scientist. He was a great man as well. He was correct in saying that he had learned "besides science something of the ends of life, something about withering and blooming . . . ." Probably without this knowledge no man is ever great. Without it no man can be anything more than a skillful machine. And with it . . . ?

With it there are men like Noguchi, who would play chess with a friend until two o'clock in the morning and then go back to the laboratory to work through the remainder of the night. With it Noguchi would master languages—English, French, German, Chinese, Danish, Italian, Spanish, Russian—with the same intensity he displayed in mastering knowledge of species of bacteria. He would paint forcefully or fish wildly in the little stream behind his summer cottage in the Catskills. Then he would turn with equal passion to his test tubes. He would listen to his wife reading *The Kreutzer Sonata* to him while he examined slides bearing diseased tissue from the human brain. He would find the book abominable and be able to say why. And in the two-hundredth slide he would find the cause of a fatal disease, a spiral bacteria which no one else had been able to locate.

If Noguchi's ideal was "narrow and small" when he first came to America, certainly it grew enormously while he was here. As he said, he learned something of the ends of life. And, having learned, perhaps he was still able to say, as he watched the progress in his own body of the disease he had observed so often in others, "There is some good fate in how my affairs are, and my research is entering a sweet realm."

Albert Einstein

A GERMAN Jew—Albert Einstein, theoretical physicist, one of the greatest thinkers of all time and one
of the greatest geniuses of the modern world—became
an American citizen in 1940, and the United States may
well be proud of this searcher after truth. Experiments
and measurements he always left to other physicists,
while he observed, imagined, *thought*. And his thought
has caused a revolution in scientific ideas.

When he was a very little boy, Albert was thought by
his parents to be mentally deficient because his mental
processes seemed backward and the power of speech
came slowly. They seem to have been ordinary towns-
people to whom the child was born in 1879 at Ulm,
Germany. A year later the family moved to Munich.
The father carried on an electrical business and was interested in engineering. He was of a kindly, optimistic
nature, but he never made a great success. He had renounced the Jewish faith and was a materialist in
thought. The mother, more serious in some ways but
with a sense of humor, was a lover of people and devoted to her family. The only apparent likeness between

mother and son was a love of music. At six years of age
Albert played the violin and at twelve had a passion for
music beyond his years, playing mostly Mozart, Beethoven, and Bach. This love stayed with him throughout
his life and was always his solace and recreation.

The schools of Munich had little educational ideal;
they were crude, severe, and compulsory in method, and
as a boy Albert Einstein hated classes. He felt alone with
an "inner loneliness"; he found little sympathy at home,
and in school he had a feeling of isolation and did not
associate with his schoolmates. Dr. Max Talmy writes
that he felt it his good fortune to come in contact with
this boy who was then ten years old. For five years they
were intimate friends. He gave Albert a book on physics
and his first book on mathematics. He comments:
"When Albert was about thirteen the flight of his mathematical genius was so high and swift I could no longer
follow him." They turned to philosophy, and Immanuel
Kant, incomprehensible to many adults, but "clear to
this young schoolboy." His first geometry excited him,
and he went on eagerly to other branches of mathematics. He never excelled in languages or in anything that
called for memorizing. But now his teachers recognized
his ability, and he was considered a genius. For years he
had felt a growing love of nature; in his long lone walks
its wonders and its beauties had developed a true reverence in him. As a little child Albert showed a religious
interest, largely due to this association with nature. He is

reported to have composed songs of praise to God and to have sung them at home and on the street. In early adolescence his religious feeling was related to music and other forms of art in which he had an increasing interest. Later, other interests supplanted that of religion, except that in adult life it expressed itself in what Dr. Einstein termed cosmic religion.

When he was sixteen years of age his father's business failed. The family decided to venture anew in Milan, Italy. This led to a great and delightful change for young Einstein. He was allowed six months' freedom from schooling and spent his time in art museums, in reading, and in seeing the natural beauties of Italy, which he loved. He lived in a dream and was little fitted for ordinary pursuits. His chief desire was to be free. He renounced his German citizenship and cared little for his Jewish heritage. Finally, he was sent to Switzerland to take entrance examinations at Zurich Academy. In these he failed, and necessity forced him to go to a lower school. In its liberal atmosphere he was happy, and in a year's time he was enabled to enter the Academy.

For some time there had been growing a great change in his mental interest and attitude. He became indifferent to mathematics and turned to philosophy rather than science, except for his devotion to physics. He read with avidity the works of the great physicists and at this period sought empirical methods for the solution of problems. He showed an intellectual hunger for knowledge, but the methods of the lecture room bored him, and he cut many of his classes, though the college had some famous teachers. Einstein lived in solitude on a small income and often was undernourished. A few kindred spirits became his friends: Marcel Grossman, an able woman who studied with him and years later assisted him in working out his theories; the Austrian socialist, Friedrich Adler, who was a physicist and seemed to Einstein a pure idealist. He read also with Mileva Maric, a Serbian, who afterward became his first wife. In later life he married a widowed cousin, Elsa, with whom he had played in childhood. She died in 1936.

Upon graduation, Einstein's father planned for him to seek an engineering position. This was abhorrent to the son. It was, however, necessary for him to earn his living. After attempts at tutoring in a struggle to earn enough to keep himself alive, he felt more keenly the injustices of life which he had observed as a child. He had noted then the unjust discrimination against the poor. Now he felt it personally.

At the age of twenty-three he obtained a position at the Patent Office of Berne. This work required insight and judgment, and he liked it; also it allowed opportunity to pursue his investigations in physics. While there Einstein developed and published his theory of relativity in its restricted form—the remarkable achievement of a scientific imagination. In his excitement over this and other discoveries in physics he exclaimed, "It was as if a

storm had broken loose in my head!" During this time
he took his Ph.D. from Zurich University. And while at
Berne he married, and a son was born to him. His life
satisfied him now, and he was content to remain where
he was. In his student days he had become a citizen of
Switzerland. By 1909, however, Einstein's writings were
known, and through the influence of one of his old professors he was appointed extraordinary professor of theo-
retic physics at the University of Zurich. He was invited
to lecture in several European cities, then accepted the
chair of physics at Prague University in 1911. Two years
later Professor Einstein was urged to return to Zurich,
this time to a full professorship in his old Polytechnic
Academy. From there he went to Berlin. His ability was
so generally recognized that a special position was created for him as director of the Kaiser Wilhelm Physical
Institute. He was elected a member of the Royal Prus-
sian Academy of Sciences and received an income sufficient to allow him to devote much time to research.

In 1915 Dr. Einstein put forth his *General Theory of
Relativity,* and at the celebration of his fiftieth anniversary, Professor A. A. Michelson, a world-famous scientist, said, "Dr. Einstein's theory of relativity has caused a
revolution in scientific thought unprecedented in the
history of science." In his modest, unobtrusive way, Einstein turned to Michelson, saying, "It was you who led
the physicists into new paths, and through your marvel-

ous experimental work paved the way for the development of the theory of relativity; it was your verifications which first set the theory on a real basis." The physicist, Robert Millikan, said on this occasion, "You can throw general relativity into the wastebasket if you will, and Professor Einstein's position as the leading mind in the development of our modern physics would still remain unchallenged." This was said in an important magazine fifteen years later: "The main achievement of the general theory of relativity is that it has advanced a uniformity of view of the physical world structure."

In an interesting article (*Forum*, October, 1930) entitled "What I Believe," Dr. Einstein said:

> Many times a day I realize how much my own outer and inner life is built upon the labors of my fellow men both living and dead, and how earnestly I must exert myself in order to give in return as much as I have received. My peace of mind is often troubled by the depressing sense that I have borrowed too heavily from the work of other men . . . . Without the sense of collaborating with like-minded beings in the pursuit of the ever unattainable in art and scientific research, my life would have been empty.

Yet Dr. Einstein loved solitude and cared little for ordinary social contacts, saying of himself, "My passionate interest in social justice and social responsibility has always stood in curious contrast to a marked lack of desire for direct association with men and women. I am a horse for single harness, not cut out for tandem or team work."

Like some other geniuses, he was careless as to appearances. He hated publicity too. When newspaper men and crowds of people assembled to greet him on arrival in America, he tried to get away, saying in his shy, embarrassed manner, *"Why* do they do it?" He had a soft voice and kindly eye and smile but sometimes grew irate under annoyance and interruption. Humility, sincerity, and integrity were his striking characteristics. It has been said, "No one can meet Professor Einstein for the first time without an immediate realization of extraordinary intellectual power combined with a natural simplicity and kindliness which so often characterizes great genius."

The honors conferred upon Dr. Einstein were many. The leading universities of Europe gave him degrees, and several scientific academies elected him to membership. In 1921 he was awarded the Nobel prize; the Copley medal of the Royal Society was presented to him in 1925; and in 1926 the Royal Astronomical Society of London bestowed on him its highest distinction, the gold medal. He expressed his gratitude to this Society in these words:

> The man who has discovered an idea which allows us to penetrate, to whatever slight degree, a little more deeply the eternal mystery of nature has been allotted a

great share of grace. If, in addition, he experiences the best help, sympathy and recognition of his time, he attains almost more happiness than one man can bear.

Help, sympathy, and recognition were not forthcoming from all quarters, however. Dr. Einstein's happiness was leavened with rage and woe when the Nazis came to power in Germany. Hitler and his brutal minions were incapable of sympathy and respect, and they helped only themselves. One of the things they helped themselves to was a sum of money that Albert Einstein had on deposit in Germany. Their justification for this theft—confiscation, they called it—was that Einstein was a Jew and an intellectual.

The Nazis were particularly vicious in their treatment of Jews. Their outrages caused Dr. Einstein to identify himself more closely with the Jewish people. Eagerly assisting the Jews in every way possible, he encouraged them to help themselves through peaceful self-assertion as a national unit among the nations of the world. A strong believer in Zionism, he was an influential supporter of the movement which resulted in the establishment of Israel.

The greatest thinker of our time, Dr. Einstein actively fostered free thought. He helped to establish and carry on the Hebrew University in Jerusalem, expressing the hope that "our University will always be free from a spirit of narrow nationalism, that teachers and students will always preserve the consciousness that they serve their people best when they maintain its union with humanity and with the highest human values." In America, too, Dr. Einstein spoke out against the narrow nationalism that would destroy our freedom while loudly proclaiming its glories.

From childhood Einstein had a horror of war and all that is involved in it. He called himself a militant pacifist. He despised war and had a contempt for the man who marches to music to kill another. "I would rather," he said, "be smitten to shreds than participate in such doings." His political ideal was democracy, and during his later years he made his home in Princeton, New Jersey, where he was a member of The Institute for Advanced Study.

When he was asked some years ago for a formula for success in life he replied, "If A is success in life, I should say the formula is $A = X + Y + Z$, X being work and Y being play." "And what is Z?" he was asked. "That," he answered, "is keeping your mouth shut."

Dr. Einstein's religious views were indicative of the man. He said:

Everything that men do or think concerns the satisfaction of the needs they feel, or the escape from pain. This must be kept in mind when we seek to understand spiritual or intellectual movements and the way in which they develop. For feeling and longing are the motive forces of all human striving and productivity—however nobly these latter may display themselves to us. What then are the feelings and the needs which have brought mankind to religious thought and to faith in the widest sense? A moment's consideration shows that the most varied emotions stand at the cradle of religious thought and experience. In primitive peoples it is, first of all, fear that awakens religious ideas—fear of hunger, of wild animals, of illness and of death. A second source of religious development is found in the social feelings. The longing for guidance, for love and succor, provides the stimulus for the growth of a social or moral conception of God. This is the God of Providence who protects, decides, rewards and punishes . . . . This is the social or moral idea of God. Only exceptionally gifted individuals or especially noble communities rise essentially above this level; in these there is found a third level of religious experience. I will call it the cosmic religious sense. This is hard to make clear to those who do not experience it, since it does not involve an anthropomorphic idea of God; the individual feels the vanity of human desires and aims, and the nobility and marvelous order which are revealed in nature and in the world of thought.

Again he said:

The most beautiful thing we can experience is the mysterious. It is the source of all true art and science. He to whom this emotion is a stranger, who can no longer pause to wonder and stand rapt in awe, is as good as dead: his eyes are closed. This insight into the mystery of life, coupled though it be with fear, has also given rise to religion. To know that what is impenetrable to us really exists, manifesting itself as the highest wisdom and the most radiant beauty which our dull faculties can comprehend only in their most primitive forms—this knowledge, this feeling, is at the center of true religiousness. In this sense and in this sense only, I belong in the ranks of devoutly religious men.

Dr. Einstein died at the age of seventy-six, on April 18, 1955.

Hans Hofmann

WHEN Hans Hofmann invented an electromagnetic comptometer in 1896, at the age of sixteen, his father, Theodor, fairly burst with pride. He predicted that Hans would be a famous scientist and that people would remember his son for all his wonderful inventions.

His predictions could not have been wider from the mark, for Hans Hofmann grew up to be one of the most influential painters and art teachers of twentieth-century America. When he died on February 17, 1966, at the grand old age of eighty-six in his Greenwich Village apartment in New York City, Hans Hofmann was hailed for his great role in helping American artists emerge as a decisive influence on the international art scene.

Hans was born on March 21, 1880, in the little Bavarian village of Weissenburg. He was one of five children. His father worked for the Bavarian government. His mother, Franciska, was the daughter of Frederik Manger, a prominent brewer and wine-producer. When

Hans was six, his family moved to Munich, but he spent summers at Grosspapa Manger's farm.

On hot, lazy afternoons, the boy would go down to the Altmuehthal barge canal that wound through the fields and watch the water from a tree-shaded spot. When the water was motionless, he saw a perfect reflection of the opposite canal bank; but the reflection was broken up when the barges came by rippling the waters. In later years he would be concerned with light, color, and images.

When he was sixteen, his father got him a job as an engineering assistant in the office of the Director of Public Works of Bavaria, and Hans left his father's house to live by himself. He applied himself to the books in the engineering library and soon had invented the electromagnetic comptometer. Shortly afterwards, Theodor sent his son a thousand marks, a reward of sorts for his achievement. Hans deposited the money in a bank and decided on the study of art to occupy his leisure time.

Hans continued to invent devices. He sensitized a light bulb so that it drew power from the earth's magnetism and did not need electric current. It would have made an ideal lamp for miners, if only its light hadn't been so dim. He invented a portable freezing unit, too. And in 1898, when the papers were full of news of a shipwreck, the young man invented a radarlike underwater signal to warn vessels of unseen dangers.

But it was art that claimed him. Oh, he chafed under

the discipline of mediocre teachers, and the so-called rules of art sometimes seemed very limiting to him. But Hofmann stuck to it, learning to sketch and paint according to old traditions.

Meanwhile, he met Maria Wolfegg, whom everyone called "Miz," and married her. They never had children, but their love and marriage lasted until Miz died in 1963. One of the very few of Hofmann's early works which survived World War I was a portrait of Miz, done in 1901.

Then one day, Hofmann's horizons widened considerably when Willi Schwartz, a painter, came back to Munich from Paris. Willi told Hans of the exciting ideas of the Post-Impressionists, how they were more interested in the light reflected from objects than in the objects themselves, how they could get wonderful effects in their paintings by placing swabs, and even tiny points, of pure color next to each other on the canvas, rather than blending the colors.

Hofmann was impressed with Paul Cézanne's notion that "when color is richest, form is fullest," and he began to paint in the Impressionist style. Another early work of Hofmann that has survived is a self-portrait in this style.

Willi Schwartz liked what Hofmann was doing and arranged for him to meet Philip Freudenberg, a wealthy Berlin department store owner and art collector. Freudenberg was so impressed by Hofmann's talent that he insisted on sending Hofmann and his wife to Paris, paying their train fare and promising to support them while Hans studied and painted.

And so it was that one wintry morning in 1904, Hans and Miz arrived in Paris just at the beginning of one of the most explosive and fertile periods in art history. They climbed up one of the streets of Montparnasse on the way to their new home. Chilled by the cold winter wind, they stopped in a restaurant near the summit of Montparnasse for some hot coffee. Not knowing much French, Hans managed by sign language to get the waiter to bring them some bread. The waiter brought them croissants, which they found delicious, and they returned again and again to the café.

It happened that the restaurant, the Café du Dôme, was a favorite meeting place for many of the young artists in Paris. What arguments they used to have! There were painters of all nations there—the Frenchmen, Georges Braque, Henri Matisse, and Robert Delaunay, who became Hofmann's closest friend; the Spaniards, Pablo Picasso and Juan Gris; and there were Norwegians and Dutch and Americans. The arguments were all about the old "rules" and the new theories of art.

It was all very well for the "older" generation, the Impressionists, to be concerned with the light reflected from objects and to paint in pure colors. But some of the younger artists chose to mix colors again. Some wanted to bathe their canvasses in broad sweeps of color when they painted objects, rather than paint in tiny swabs of it. Still others argued that the Impressionists, for all their attempts to avoid photographic renditions of their models, were still too "representational." That is, a bowl of fruit looked like a bowl of fruit; landscapes and buildings and people looked just like landscapes and buildings and people. The new generation wanted to "abstract" the forms of objects, that is, go beneath the surfaces of things and paint the essences of fruit bowls and buildings. Some worked hard to get the illusion of motion in their paintings. They argued and they painted and they argued and they painted, and Hans Hofmann was part of all the ferment.

The year after Hans and Miz came to Paris, a group of his friends exhibited their paintings together in the Autumn Salon. The next day, one journalist severely criticized the group, saying that he had felt surrounded by *fauves,* that is, wild beasts. The name stuck, and the group's movement was called *Fauvism.* Among the *fauves* were Matisse, Maurice Vlaminck, Maurice Utrillo, Raoul Dufy, and Georges Rouault.

Then in 1908, Picasso and Braque made their first experiments with purely abstract form, a technique that became known as Cubism.

The Cubists shrugged at color; they were more interested in the forms of things. They saw objects in terms of planes and areas, rather than of lines. Perspective was gradually discarded, and pictures became purely two dimensional.

In his own painting, Hans Hofmann was more of an observer of this ferment than a participant. He merely "flirted" with the ideas that so intrigued his friends. As he was to say in later years, "It was a rather platonic affair." Most of his paintings were still lifes, landscapes in the Luxembourg Gardens, and figure pieces. But the ferment of Paris stayed in his mind. All the contradictory theories simmered in his soul, until they exploded many years later in America. Hofmann would be recognized as the leading force of what is now known as "Abstract Expressionism."

In 1909 Hofmann had his first one-man show at the Neue Secession Gallery in Berlin. The next year, his second was held in Paul Cassirer's Gallery, also in Berlin. His Parisian friends were impressed, since none of them had had the honor of one-man shows yet. They had only exhibited in groups. His patron, Philip Freudenberg, who had been supporting him all this time in Paris, was pleased with his work.

Hofmann then suffered a serious lung ailment and he and Miz went to Corsica to regain his health. When the couple were in Munich for a brief vacation before returning to Paris, World War I broke out. Almost all of Hans's paintings were in Paris! He couldn't get back, and he couldn't get the paintings out of France. They

were lost forever. Meanwhile, Freudenberg stopped supporting him. The German army rejected him for military service because of the after-effects of his lung ailment.

He was now thirty-four years old. His world had
fallen apart. The shock of losing all his paintings, the
dislocation which the war forced on him, and the fact
that he needed an income to support himself and Miz
led him to open up an art school in the Munich suburb
of Schwabing, the Hans Hofmann Schule für moderne
Kunst, the School of Modern Art. He soon had about a
hundred students, mostly women.

After the war, Hofmann's fame as a teacher spread.
His students came from all parts of Europe and some
came from the United States. Georgenstrasse 40 became
the 10 Downing Street of the art world. The pressures
of his classes kept him from doing much painting himself. But he talked with his students about the various
techniques of the Impressionists, Fauves, and Cubists;
the Expressionism of Paul Klee, and the abstract geome-
tries of Piet Mondrian and Vasili Kandinski. He let his
students paint however they liked, in abstract or in traditional representational forms. But what he tried to
teach them was the concept of space, spatial relationships, opposing spatial tensions among objects.

"Draw a line on a sheet of paper," he would say. "It
tells you nothing of length, direction or form. Now
draw another, shorter line at an angle to the first line.

You know now the first line is longer, is moving in a direction related to the second line and influenced by the second line, and you can see the beginning of form. Relate these tensions to the borders of your paper and a whole new series of relationships appears."

Hofmann would apply the same insights to planes and then to color. But, above all, the entire process of painting was to him an "expression" of the artist himself. In 1961 he was to say, "My paintings are always images of my whole psychic makeup. You cannot deny yourself. You ask, am I painting myself? I'd be a swindler, if I did otherwise. I'd be denying my existence as an artist."

In 1930 two of his former students, Professors Worth Ryder and Glenn Wessels of the art department of the University of California, persuaded Hofmann to teach summer sessions at the Berkeley campus. Not long after he arrived, he received a letter from Miz telling him of Adolf Hitler's election victory in Germany. "Stay in America," she advised. "I will join you there."

It was a difficult decision to make. Give up his Munich school? Completely cut his ties and start afresh a second time? He was already fifty-one! Samuel Kootz, Hofmann's art dealer and friend from 1947 until the artist's death in 1966, says that Hofmann knew Hitler would suppress him in Germany—the fate that befell other artists and teachers who stayed. His whole teaching career had been based on the notion of freeing the artist to be true to his inner vision. He knew this would be impossible in a totalitarian state.

So Miz came to America, too, and that fall, Hofmann taught classes at the Art Students League in New York. In the summers of 1932 and 1933, he taught at the Thurn School in Gloucester, Massachusetts. He re-established his Munich school in Greenwich Village in New York in the fall of 1932, and in 1934, started his own summer classes at Provincetown on Cape Cod, Massachusetts.

More important, he started painting in oils again, mostly still lifes and landscapes. But he did not exhibit his new paintings until 1941, when the Isaac Delgado Museum in New Orleans gave him a one-man show.

In the meantime, he had painted "Red Trickle" in 1939 and "Poet" in 1940. "Red Trickle" was the first application of what is known as the "drip technique" to painting, a technique of dripping paint instead of brushing it on to a canvas, which has been used since then so successfully by Jackson Pollock. With "Poet," Hofmann moved toward complete abstraction.

He was sixty-four years old when he gave his first one-man show in New York, at Peggy Guggenheim's Art of This Century Gallery. In the succeeding twenty-one years, he turned out an enormous number of paintings. Even his hostile critics stood in awe of his energy. The New York art world was slow to accept him and even now critics are divided on his place as an artist. But as a teacher, they are nearly unanimous in calling him the dominant influence in American art during the thirties, forties, and fifties. After all, he had taught some six thousand students in that time, a great many of whom went on to become famous in their own right. Others became teachers themselves, spreading his gospel of individualism in art.

But that first New York show in 1944 did not get rave reviews. His paintings were dismissed as "improvisations." Beginning in 1947, he exhibited his new paintings annually at the Kootz Gallery, on New York's Madison Avenue. In 1948 the Addison Gallery of American Art in Andover, Massachusetts, gave him his first "retrospective" exhibit, a display of paintings done over a number of years that showed the artist's development.

From April to June 1957, the Whitney Museum of American Art, a leading force in the art world, finally did the same for him. The fifty-five oils and twenty-one watercolors and drawings then toured major museums in the country. In 1958 he gave up his school to devote full time to his painting—at the age of seventy-eight!

Critics saw three stages in his development: works done directly from nature; works based on the geometrical structures of cubism; and works displaying increasingly free forms. "Truro River," 1937, exemplified his nature studies; "Magenta and Blue," 1950, cubism; and

"Orchestral Dominance in Yellow," 1954, and "X-1955," the free forms.

Harold Rosenberg, *Art News* critic, said, "No American artist could mount a show of greater coherent variety. His originality suggests no limits."

As if to prove this point, in addition to his annual shows at the Kootz Gallery, Hofmann held a third comprehensive exhibition in 1963. Thirty-six of the forty paintings shown had been done after he was seventy-four years old.

Calling the exhibition "extraordinary," the *New York Times* critic Brian O'Doherty said that Hofmann "is painting better than ever in the last decade. His painting never looked more youthful or spontaneous. The most delightful aspect of this show is its irrepressible joyousness—a joyousness that runs from pungent strength to rather overlight lyricism . . . they are paintings that wither both scholarship and history by their superb presence."

But Emily Genauer, the New York *Herald Tribune* critic, dissented. She believed that the art movement Hofmann had started in America, Abstract Expressionism, had run its course, and that by continuing to paint in the purely abstract style, Hofmann was in a blind alley. Criticizing one painting in the 1963 show, "Delirious Pink," done in 1961, Emily Genauer described it as "several swabs of pink, plus one of umber and black on a white ground. Its effect is not unlike that of samples of lipstick smeared on paper (could Hofmann have had his tongue in his cheek when he gave his picture its beauty-salon title?). It's a school-room exercise in surface tensions."

Thomas B. Hess, a friendly critic and the editor of *Art News,* later replied that Hofmann, despite his happy nature, never joked about or with his painting: "He had an aristocratic contempt for tact and understatement; he is never ironic. When he wants to signal, he blasts the trombone. When he wants to murmur, he becomes a turtle-dove as big as the Ritz."

For Hofmann, the significance of a painting lay in the balance of opposing forces. Objects occupied space and the space between objects was filled with forces and tensions that held objects in *their* spaces. Objects made forms in space and when they moved, other "forms" —objects or space itself—took up the place or area that had been occupied. Hofmann "saw" the forces and tensions among objects and tried to depict them on canvas. The objects themselves were no longer important in themselves, but only in their relationships with each other. Like the images in the Altmuehthal barge canal that were broken up by the force of an approaching barge. Like the earth's magnetic forces, which had made the device he had invented glow dimly. Like the intervals between notes of music. As he said to his students, art was a "constant process of push answering pull, and pull answering push."

And the way to show those relationships, Hofmann felt, was through color. As critic O'Doherty observed: "He has the warmest, coarsest, most opulent color sense of any modern painter."

Hofmann himself said, "Color is the greatest plastic means. Every color makes a new form . . . . Painting means forming with color," and his oils were "like violins and flutes that I must orchestrate into a symphony . . . our entire being is nourished by color . . . . I want always to live in color."

And he did! His home in Provincetown was a wild paradise of color. He and Miz painted one wide-boarded floor bright green, another floor a blinding red, still another floor sun-yellow. There were green chairs, yellow chairs, pure white chairs. There was a round, orangey-red side table with a lucent blue bowl into which Miz daily put fresh flowers—perhaps daisies, perhaps sunflowers—from the garden outside. There was a purple chest of drawers. The stairwell walls were yellow and the stairs themselves were blue, green, and white. The white walls in most of the rooms were hung with Hofmann's brilliant paintings. When the sunlight poured in there was no chance for gloom.

And indeed, Hans Hofmann was never a gloomy man. He was the essence of cheerfulness. Some of his students called him "Santa Claus"—he looked like a tall, husky Santa, without the whiskers, but with white hair, a crinkled, kindly face, the sun cascading from his laughing blue eyes. As one critic put it: "He did not make gifts, but his booming presence could scatter a glitter of Bavarian snowflakes in the dampest, hottest Cape Cod afternoon . . . . He gave abundantly of his energy and affection to a raw, shaky milieu" [the new generation of American artists who needed his direction and encouragement].

What Hofmann gave his students was a sense of security and belief in themselves. When he came here in the Thirties, American artists were really at a crossroads. Cubism, Fauvism, Surrealism had their high priests in Europe and their imitators in America. Hofmann came along with a new synthesis and the movement was called "Abstract Expressionism." Hofmann made rules, but they were often contradictory. Yet, despite his great success as an art teacher, he always maintained that art could not be taught—"all you can do is try to bring out in the individual whatever you think can be brought out. All a school can do is *not* stifle talent."

When Hofmann *taught,* he worked very hard, emerging from a class perspiring and exhausted. His juggernaut frame would move from one student to the next, talking, discussing, arguing, cajoling, pointing out this good effect or that bad stroke or color. "See what you could have done," he would say, as he painted over what the student had done or cut up the student's work and rearranged the pieces. Or he might look over someone's shoulder and say, "Your palette is more beautiful than your picture." But he said it in a kindly way, always urging the student toward an ideal that he knew intuitively, but which he sometimes could not communicate.

When Hofmann *painted,* he was just as restless and physically active, even in his eighties. Elaine de Kooning describes how he would apply paint with broad, lunging gestures, never sitting down, constantly moving from palette to easel, often finishing a painting in a few hours. "Making a picture is almost physical struggle with me," he said.

He rarely had a preconceived idea of what it was he would paint. "My work is not accidental and is not planned," he said. "The first red spot on a white canvas may at once suggest to me the meaning of 'morning redness' and from there on I dream further with my color."

But it was not an actual morning that Hofmann painted. His early portraits, landscapes, and still lifes show that he was a master of line and could draw quite skillfully in the traditional way. But from the Forties on, he was interested in non-representational painting. In his abstractions, the process itself became the goal. Each painting grew and developed according to its own logic and organic unity.

"At the time of making a picture, I want not to know

what I'm doing; a picture should be made with feeling, not with knowing. The possibilities of the medium must be sensed. Anything can serve as a medium—kerosene, benzene, turpentine, linseed oil, beeswax . . ." and with a laugh, "even beer."

Hofmann was grateful to the United States, of which he had become a citizen in 1941. In America, he said, "I can unfold all the possibilities of my mind."

He wanted to show that gratitude in some way, and when Miz died in 1963, his good friend, Kootz, suggested that he set up a memorial for her at the University of California. It was the university which, by letting him teach there for two summers, had "rescued" him from Nazi Germany, a place where his creativity and his career would have suffered.

So he gave the university a free choice of forty-five of his works plus $250,000 for the Hans and Maria Hofmann Memorial Galleries, a wing of an art museum that the university would build on its Berkeley campus.

This he could easily afford, for in the last decade of his life, each of his new paintings sold for thousands of dollars and his fertile brush produced enough pictures to bring in more than $200,000 a year.

At Hofmann's last show, held in February of 1966, Robert W. White, of the *Herald Tribune,* "noted with awe" Hofmann's "vitality" at the age of eighty-five, and said his paintings were "freer, airier, more vibrant than ever." All but two of the twenty-one large oils in his last show at the Kootz Gallery had been done within the preceding year.

There seemed to be no end to the man's vigor. He had remarried in the previous summer. His second wife was a young woman, Renate Schmitz, whom he had met at a social gathering. And Kootz says that he painted most days from six in the morning, or when the first light came, until six at night. Except for a touch of arthritis in the leg, there was nothing wrong with him. And then he died suddenly in his apartment on February 17, 1966, apparently of a heart attack.

"I cannot understand how anyone is able to paint without optimism," he used to say. "Despite the general pessimistic attitude in the world today, I am nothing but an optimist . . . . I am an optimist multiplicated one thousand times. I do not like Weltschmerz in art. Art should provide enjoyment . . . . I bring the landscape home in me."

And the landscape brought Hans Hofmann home to it. He was buried in Provincetown, where he had spent so many summers teaching others, where he had walked so often among the bright cornflowers and phlox that his beloved Miz had planted in the front yard, where he had dreamed so many hours among the yellow dunes watching the changing sunlight and the deep blues and greens of the Atlantic Ocean.

Walter Gropius

WHEN the Boston Institute of Contemporary Art displayed models and photographs of the work of Walter Gropius, in a retrospective exhibition in 1952, one popular magazine commented on the surprisingly small number of buildings that this extremely influential architect had erected. With so few buildings to his credit, how could this man have acquired his reputation as one of the foremost of contemporary architects? The answer to this question is provided by an examination of the career of the man who for over thirty-four years had been one of architecture's greatest thinkers and teachers. As founder and director of Germany's *Bauhaus,* which means literally the "house of building," and, later, in America, as head of Harvard's Graduate School of Design, Gropius had developed two of the outstanding architectural schools of modern times. Thousands of students had flocked to these schools to listen to the progressive ideas of Professor Gropius. Later, as architects, they expressed in stone and glass, steel and cement, the modern concepts they had assimilated in the classroom under the master. A new era in architecture had resulted, an era in which the materials and machines of modern industrialism and mass production were fully utilized for the first time in buildings designed to combine usefulness and beauty.

There was yet another reason why the number of buildings that could be called Gropius' was few. The contribution that Gropius has made to modern architecture is as much an attitude as a style. He has been called the "Great Collaborator," and much of his best work exists not in isolated singularity, but as part of the joint effort of fellow architects and students. He firmly believes that the integrated work of a group has a greater potential value than the sum of the work of its members when they work separately. Regarding architecture as "an interpretation of life," he feels that the design of a building should reflect the "intellectual, social, and technical conditions of our time." These conditions create a demand for certain kinds of buildings—factories, for instance, and large-scale housing developments. And the demand is best met, according to Gropius, not by the creative individual anxious to put the stamp of his own personality on his work, but by the co-operative effort of a number of people equally in touch with the conditions. Thus the architect "is to be the brother of the engineer and the manufacturer," whose roles are as important as his own in determining the form that a building will take. The architect's role is distinctive only insofar as he organizes, or puts together in a meaningful whole.

the ideas which his brother workers hold in common.

This man, who has so greatly influenced those who are doing our building today, was born in Berlin, Germany, on May 18, 1883. His father, Walter, Sr., was a surveyor in a Berlin suburb. His mother was a lively, intelligent woman who often discussed with young Walter the long tradition of architecture and painting in the Gropius family. At an early age the boy determined upon a career as an architect, and upon his graduation from the gymnasium, or secondary school, in 1903, he promptly enrolled in a technical school in Munich. He progressed rapidly at Munich and was recognized as an exceptional student, but he soon had to leave school for his required military training. Joining a regiment of hussars in 1904, he rose to the rank of corporal in a short time and, before leaving the regiment at the expiration of his period of service, he had been made a Vice-Sergeant Major.

When he was able to return to school, he attended the Berlin Technische Hochschule, an advanced technical school, from 1905 to 1907. It was during this period of training that the young student executed his first independent buildings, being commissioned by his uncle to design some houses for the workmen on his estate in Pomerania. Upon graduating, Walter spent some time visiting Spain, Italy, and England. Returning to Berlin in 1908, he was appointed head assistant to Professor

Peter Behrens, one of his former instructors at the Technische Hochschule.

In 1910 Gropius temporarily abandoned teaching in order to practice architecture. He soon won several commissions, including a factory for the Fagus Shoe Company at Alfeld and settlements for workers at Wittenberg and Frankfort. This early work was distinguished by the use of what were then unusual new building materials. Such things as concrete, aluminum, stainless steel, and great expanses of shining glass were used with great effectiveness. The lines of the buildings were clean and functional, in keeping with the materials employed. Gropius did not clutter his structures with the customary but unnecessary columns, arches, and porches, or with the dull statuary and stone carving so common at the time. Instead, he let his new materials speak for themselves. And they did so eloquently: the bright sparkle of glass; the smooth, urbane gleam of polished steel; and the sinuous curve or stern, sharp angle of poured concrete. So unusual was the work that Gropius was in great demand. He was immediately employed upon several private residences. Later he completed an outstanding group of factories and offices in Cologne.

Soon other architects began to use the materials and methods that Gropius had introduced. A group of them, bound together by certain common characteristics, became known as the creators of a distinctive style: the International Style. Its most important early exponents were Le Corbusier, who was French, Mies Van der Rohe and J. J. P. Oud, who were both Dutch, and Gropius, who, of course, was German. The techniques of the International Style, like its practitioners, were thus not the product of a single country, as the architectural techniques of ancient Greece or Rome or of French Gothic or English Tudor had been. The industrial revolution had been an international development, and its exploitation for serious artistic ends was the aim of this group of architects. These men refused to obscure their new materials with unnecessary decoration, since the textures and forms they worked in were sufficiently decorative in themselves. Nor would they force their designs to conform to a symmetrical scheme, with doors, windows, beams, and pillars formally arranged in a rigid pattern. Instead, they emphasized the rhythms set up by the functional disposition of the building's elements: equally spaced horizontal girders, encircling bands of masonry, the position of such things as elevator shafts and exits and entrances. Moreover, with skeletal steel frameworks, walls no longer had to be massive affairs. They became protective sheaths, often mere curtains of glass delimiting an interior space and permitting a new relationship between the building and its inhabitants and its environment.

It can be seen that it was not alone with the tools and materials created by the industrial revolution that these men were concerned. They were concerned also with the new relationships which that great event had brought about. With man's control over nature increasing, he was able to live at peace with it, no longer hiding behind thick stone walls from sunlight, fresh air, and growing things. And the relationships of men with one another were changing too, though more slowly. Consequently, Gropius and the men of vision responsible for the development of the International Style directed their attention toward the new architectural problems of an industrial age: mass, low-cost housing for workers; safe, efficient factories; spacious stores; comfortable, well-lit offices.

Unfortunately, the activities of Gropius and his fellow artists were soon interrupted by another consequence of the industrial revolution—World War I. Gropius was called up by the German Army. Commissioned as a lieutenant, he was put into a reserve regiment, the Ninth Hussars. At this time Gropius married, but he was able to spend little time with his wife, for his regiment was soon moved to the front lines, where Gropius was wounded in action and was awarded the Mark of Distinction. When he was released from service in 1918, his medals included the Austrian Royal Distinction, the Military Medal of Merit, and the Iron Cross, first and second class.

Before the war Gropius had belonged to the *Deutsche Werkbund*, a craft organization whose purpose had been "to ennoble industrial labor through the co-operation of art, industry, and handicraft." In 1919 he was appointed director of the Staatliches Bauhaus, a state-sponsored school stemming from the older organization. In his book *Staatliches Bauhaus,* Gropius says that the Bauhaus "aimed at the introduction of a new educational method in art and a new artistic concept." Destroying the artist's snobbish prejudice against practical objects made for widespread, everyday use, teachers at the Bauhaus fostered a new respect for the machine and its products. Here, for the first time, students of design were given workshop training. Learning while doing, they became familiar with the materials and machines used in mass production and geared their designs to the utilization of these materials in well-made articles destined for large-scale distribution.

Under Gropius' direction, the Bauhaus was a tremendous success, attracting the foremost artists and the best craftsmen of the time. The school became a center for the creative thought of the '20's. Mies Van der Rohe joined Gropius in training young architects. Internationally famous painters like Paul Klee and Vasili Kandinski flourished there. Max Breuer, the father of modern furniture design, was on the staff. Boglar and Lindig designed pottery on a mass-production scale. Josef and Anni Albers produced exciting stained glass and magnificent new fabrics. And Bayer and Moholy-Nagy experimented with typography and abstract photography, bringing striking innovations to those fields.

In addition to his executive activities and his teaching, Gropius wrote several books expounding the principles of the Bauhaus. He also continued to build. Several tombs, houses in Berlin and Zehlendorf, a paper factory and a warehouse in Alfeld, and a town theater for Jena were all constructed during this period.

Reactionary opposition to Gropius and the Bauhaus culminated in a charge of "architectural socialism," and threats were leveled against the school and its director by the burghers of Weimar. The more enlightened citizenry of Dessau, anxious to attract the stimulating institution, offered $230,000 and the site for a new school. This offer was accepted, and Gropius designed the new buildings in which the school was to be housed. The famous glass-walled workshop, an outstanding example of the International Style, attracted a great deal of attention when it was dedicated on December 4, 1926. The heart of the school, it was the place where the designs created by the students were "submitted to the ultimate test of determining their adaptability to mechanical mass production."

While serving as director of the Bauhaus, Gropius was commissioned by the German Government to design a 316-unit experimental housing project in Dessau. The project is notable for its use of concrete on a mass-

production scale, and the job stimulated Gropius' interest in low-cost housing developments. Realizing that a
healthy environment could help to convert the economically underprivileged into effective and useful members
of society, Gropius severed his connection with the Bauhaus and, after a brief visit to the United States in 1928,
went to work as director of public housing for the city of
Berlin. In that city and in Spandau, Frankfort-on-Main,
and Karlsruhe, he built low-cost housing settlements of
enormous sociological significance. And from the es-
thetic point of view these developments were equally
significant. As a matter of fact, after examining these
projects H. R. Hitchcock reported in his book, *Modern
Architecture,* that Gropius did his best work when dealing with problems of social importance.

Of course, anyone who was concerned with human
beings and their problems was subject to attack in the
Germany of the 1930's. Gropius was no exception. And
when in 1934 the Bauhaus was taken over by the Nazis
as a school for their vicious leaders, he went into volun-
tary exile. He went to England first. There he collaborated with Maxwell Fry on a number of residences in
London and Kent. He designed the Village College at
Impington and submitted plans to Oxford University
for a new building for Christ Church. These latter plans
were never put into effect, an omission which the British
Architect's Journal considered "a great loss to Britain."

In 1937 Walter Gropius established permanent residence in the United States. He built a home in Lincoln, Massachusetts, for himself and his second wife, whom he had married in 1923 after his first marriage had ended in divorce. In collaboration with Marcel Breuer, formerly associated with him at the Bauhaus, he designed and built a number of residences in Massachusetts and Pennsylvania. The Hagerty house in Cohasset, the Abele house in Framingham, and the Franck house in Pittsburgh are notable examples of his work at this time. He also designed the Pennsylvania exhibit at the New York World's Fair of 1939. Black Mountain College in North Carolina and Wheaton College in Massachusetts were built according to his plans.

In 1937 Gropius joined the faculty of Harvard University as Senior Professor of Architecture. The following year he was appointed chairman of the department. Under his inspired teaching Harvard became the leading architectural center in the country, attracting students from all over the world. But Walter Gropius' service to his new country did not end with his duties at Harvard. Commissioned by the government in 1941 to design a defense housing project, he collaborated with Marcel Breuer on the 250-unit Aluminum City in New Kensington, Pennsylvania. The cost of each unit was a phenomenally low $3,280. In 1942 he designed a handsome recreation center at Key West, Florida. In 1946 he was consultant on the plan to rebuild a seven-mile-square area of Chicago's South Side slums. In 1947 he was consultant to General Lucius Clay on a plan for reconstruction work in Germany. He has developed plans for the construction of new townships along super-highways to disperse industry and population from crowded American cities. And he had designed office buildings in Chicago, Boston, and Washington, one such building in the latter city being a radical prism-shaped structure with what Gropius calls "eyebrows"—steel and glass louvres that push out horizontally as protection against Washington's scorching summer sun.

Much of the work that Gropius has done in this country has been undertaken in conjunction with the Architects' Collaborative, an organization which he founded in 1946 to further his ideal of co-operative effort in the arts. The Collaborative consists of eight members, whose joint efforts have produced some of the finest buildings of our time. It was the Architects' Collaborative that erected Harvard's magnificent $3,000,000 Graduate Center in 1950. This group of buildings, consisting of seven dormitory units connected by sheltered walks with an imposing community center, is one of the outstanding examples of academic architecture in the country.

In 1953 at the age of seventy Walter Gropius retired from the Harvard University faculty to begin a new phase of his very active life. "At long last," he said, "I am beginning to build much more than was possible in the so-often unsettled past. The coming years should be the happiest and best fulfilled of my entire life."

Since then, he has been showered with honors, awards, citations, and university degrees. In a new burst of creativity, Gropius and the Architects' Collaborative have designed or been consultants on such projects as the new $80 million University of Baghdad, the $100 million Pan Am Building in New York City, one of the largest commercial office buildings in the world, the $25 million Federal Building in Boston, the United States Embassy in Athens, a huge housing project in West Berlin for some 40,000 people, a half-dozen modern schools for Massachusetts and New Hampshire and housing developments in Boston and Lexington, Massachusetts.

Even in his eighties, Gropius fights against ugliness in man's surroundings. He continues to explain the paradox of how "teamwork for cultural integration" can result in personal freedom. Complete reliance on the machine, he says, should end in the liberation of the individual, not in making him a slave.

Dour-faced in old age, Gropius condemns the streets that are "lined for miles and miles with filling stations and restaurants" and the suburban developer who "comes along, cutting down trees, bulldozing the site, and befouling our habitat."

"What will it take," he asks, "to extricate ourselves from this merry-go-round and rise above the cloud of fake values which is smothering us?" He answers his own question by saying, "purposeful, intensive education." He calls for a change in attitude, an emphasis not on "the bigger" but on "the better." Such a change will come about when we "trigger the creative potentialities of every individual through intensified education and put ever greater emphasis on the humanities. An active participation in the arts could perhaps outbalance the negative effects of automation."

Perhaps, if we listen carefully and follow his advice, technology and the machine will be what they were always meant to be, man's tool to fashion for himself a better life, rather than man's master monsters running amok.

Philip Murray

THE stock-market crash of October 1929 signalized for most Americans the beginning of ten years of misery. In the panic that followed that calamitous event forty billion dollars in securities evaporated and millions of investors lost their life savings. Business houses closed by the thousands. Factories shut down. Banks failed. In the great depression which lasted for ten long years, hundreds of thousands of families lost their homes. At one time there were over twelve million unemployed Americans walking the streets looking in vain for any sort of work. This spectacle was particularly distressing because, as Franklin D. Roosevelt pointed out, plenty was at our doorstep, its use inhibited only by artificial restrictions masquerading as economic "laws." Poverty existed in the midst of abundance because the nation's productive capacity exceeded its capacity to buy. This was largely so because too great a share of the national income was controlled by a small percentage of the population. This income was promptly turned back into investments and savings, while farmers and workers in factory and office were unable to earn a large enough share of our national wealth to buy what they worked so hard to produce.

Fortunately, America was not without great leaders in its hour of crisis. President Roosevelt promised a "new deal" to the nation, and he implemented his promise with specific legislation. But legislation could not do everything. The workers had to organize themselves, to assume sufficient power to match the concentration of wealth which, in the hands of the few, made our economy dangerously unhealthy. Philip Murray, who had come to America from Scotland in his boyhood, provided the leadership which made that work effective. His own conception of the task was an elevated one. "Organization," he said, "fundamentally means . . . clothing and bread and butter and pictures on the walls and carpets on the floors and music in the home and enlarged opportunities for children to receive the benefits of better education. These are the fundamental things, the very roots underlying the foundation of the Congress of Industrial Organization."

Philip Murray, along with John L. Lewis and Sidney Hillman, was one of the founders of the CIO, a vigorous new type of union organization in America designed to restore the country's economic well-being by bringing about, through peaceful means, a greater balance of power between labor and industry. The unions of the CIO accomplished this great end by organizing the workers on an industry-wide basis. These industrial groupings, running horizontally through an entire industry, were a more powerful force than the older type of trade union, whose vertical groupings of the various trades within an industry could be more easily divided. Philip Murray undertook the job of organizing the steel-workers, for steel is America's basic industry and its workers had never been organized even in vertical unions. This was his first assignment with the CIO. Having been a coal man all his life, he knew little of the complex economics of steel when he undertook the job. But his mind, with that affinity for facts which made him so formidable a negotiator, soon mastered the intricacies of steel production and distribution. And his ability to relate these cold industrial statistics to the human needs of the workers—clothing, bread and butter, pictures, carpets, music, education—won him the support of his men. His success in organizing the workers of America's basic industry, according to one social historian, "made industrial unionism an accepted fact," and established the CIO as a social as well as an economic force. His tireless efforts resulted in the formation of the United Steelworkers of America, which was to be the rugged backbone of the CIO, a new force in our country's economic life.

Philip Murray, or Phil as he was known to hundreds of thousands of American workingmen, was no novice at union affairs when he took on the job of organizing the steel men in 1935. Born in Blantyre, Scotland, in

1886, he attended his first union meeting at the age of six, accompanying his father, William Murray, who worked in the coal mines and was the president of his local union. Phil's father was a Gladstonian liberal who taught him many of his own common sense attitudes toward economic problems. An Irishman who left his native country for Scotland when his liberal ideas brought him into conflict with the repressive British authorities there, William had married an Irish girl, Rose Ann Layden, whose family emigrated to Scotland for reasons similar to his own. Phil's mother died when he was but two years old, his sister Mary four, and the two children went to live with their grandfather, Alexander Layden, at Bothwell.

It was at Bothwell that Phil undertook his first union activity at the ripe age of seven. A great strike was being carried on in the Bothwell mines in 1893. It lasted for seventeen weeks, and after school every day Phil canvassed the town for food for the soup kitchens set up to feed the hungry strikers' families. Young Phil had only three more years of school, however, for at the age of ten he entered the mines himself, working full time as a breaker boy for eighty cents a day. The sum was not large, but it helped. Phil's father had remarried by this time, and the new wife brought a young daughter with her into the household. And soon there were other mouths to feed, for new children began to come. Eventually Phil was to have four half-brothers and four half-sisters in addition to his sister Mary and the little stepsister his father's new wife had brought with her.

With his family growing larger year by year, Phil's father began to think about moving again. He had heard about the wealth of America and, after a preliminary reconnaissance trip, he started out with Phil, in advance of the rest of the family, to set up a home in the new land. Phil and his father arrived in New York, and left Ellis Island on Christmas day, 1902, for the bituminous fields of western Pennsylvania. They got off the train at Irwin and, with their international union transfer cards in their pockets and all of their possessions in a small green trunk, which sixteen-year-old Phil toted on his back, they trudged seven miles through the snow to Madison, Pennsylvania, a small Westmoreland County coal town where Phil's Uncle Philip lived. There they settled down and awaited the rest of the family, who joined them the following year.

Phil got a job in the mines, shoveling enough coal to fill three mine cars a day at a dollar a car. At night he studied mathematics and economics. He paid sixty hard-earned dollars for an eighteen-month International Correspondence School Course. So diligently did he work that he completed the year-and-a-half course in six months. During mine layoffs he played soccer with the men from the pits. He enjoyed the game and played a fair outside left, but his Uncle Phil recalls that he was "too big in the feet" to be a good player. His organizational ability was apparent even then, however, and he managed several teams with some success.

When Phil was eighteen and working for the Keystone Coal and Coke Company in Westmoreland County, he discovered that he and the other men were being short-weighted by a company weight-master. He complained, and the weight-master vigorously denied the charge. As Murray used to tell the story:

> A fight ensued . . . the weight boss took a shot at me with a balance weight . . . . I hit him with a stool over the head. I happened to get the best of the argument, but I was discharged. Some 550 men went out in support of me. Mine guards were thrown around the place; my family was evicted from the company house. That was the beginning of these things that I am interested in.

As a result of young Phil's discovery he was elected president of the local union and led the men in a strike that lasted for four weeks. Finally the strike was broken through hunger. Phil was picked up by a group of deputy sheriffs, who escorted him to Pittsburgh and told him never to return to Westmoreland County.

Phil moved to Hazelkirk, a small, rough mining town south of Pittsburgh. Here he got a job in another coal mine and boarded at the old Red Onion boarding house, where four hundred miners slept in shifts. A prankster in those days, Phil took great delight in tying the toes of sleeping boarders to the bed posts. Another source of rough and ready fun was lining up an audience to watch old John McGary, a fellow miner, struggle into his new-fangled BVD's.

Not long after his arrival in wide-open Hazelkirk, young Phil won election to the job of union check-weighman, a position in which he would be responsible for seeing that the men were not cheated by the company weight-master. Returning to the Red Onion the night after the election, he took a short cut through a mule patch. Halfway across the field he was felled by a blow to the head and pummeled until he was senseless. When he regained consciousness, he dragged himself back to the Red Onion and with three friends set out in search of the 230 pounds of muscle and bone who had opposed him in the election. They found their man and thrashed him soundly. Eight years later, when Phil was elected to the Executive Board of the United Mine Workers, he met the burly miner again. The man admitted that he had been the assailant, congratulated Phil on his election, and both men had a hearty laugh over the episode.

While Phil was working in Hazelkirk he met a girl named Elizabeth Lavery. She was an orphan, her father having been killed when she was three in an explosion in the Van Voorhis mine. Phil and "Liz" Lavery were married in 1910 in the Roman Catholic Church of the Resurrection in the Monongahela City. They returned to the Lavery home for a wedding supper of crackers and cheese with "Aunt Jane," the elder sister who had raised Liz.

Encouraged by his wife, Phil became a naturalized citizen in 1911. His activities in District 5—the Pittsburgh local of the United Mine Workers—had begun upon his first arrival in Hazelkirk. Phil worked with men like Pat Fagan and Van Bittner, the president of the local, increasing his union activities through the years. "Sairving" the men, as Murray later admitted in his pleasant Scottish burr, could be dangerous business. He was once hit by a brick while going about union work. And once, while he and Van Bittner were addressing a union meeting, they were rushed by a gang of toughs and pushed into a creek. Such incidents, however, merely provided an added spice to the work of the sturdy, well-built young Murray. He plunged into union work with vigor and quickly rose in District 5, being elected to the International Board of the UMW in 1912, and in 1916 replacing Van Bittner as president of District 5 in an election that proved his popularity with the rank and file.

Murray won national recognition at the early age of thirty-one, when in 1917 he was appointed to President Woodrow Wilson's War Labor Board. In the following year he was also made a member of the National Bituminous Coal Production Commission. President Warren G. Harding continued a policy that was to become standard procedure with Chief Executives when he called on Murray for help in preventing violence in the

West Virginia mine fields in 1921. The hot-blooded
mountaineers who worked the mines were up in arms.
Having been pushed too far, they raised the flag of rebellion, took over telegraph lines, railroad junctions, and
signal houses and dared anyone to do anything about it.
Violence was imminent. Murray rushed into the thick of
things and managed to persuade the miners to put down
their squirrel guns. He narrowly escaped serious injury
on this mission, for his car slewed off a muddy road and
slid down a mountain side.

In 1920 Philip Murray was appointed to the position
of vice president of the United Mine Workers by John
L. Lewis, who had just assumed the presidency of that
organization. This was the beginning of a close twenty-
year friendship between the two men, a friendship for
which Murray has sometimes been criticized, being
called "subservient" or a mere "shadow" of Lewis. No
criticism could be more unjust. It is true that Murray
worked closely with Lewis all through the terrible
twenties. But the UMW was fighting for its life against
political pressure, economic demoralization, and the
fierce raids of the "Coal and Iron Police." Unity was essential if the union was to survive. It did survive those
terrible times largely because of the close teamwork of
its two top executives. Lewis of those days has been described as the "farseeing strategist and master of psychological warfare." A close observer has said that he would
"thunder and bluster and threaten the coal operators,
then Philip Murray would move in with his solid array

of facts. A first-rate negotiator, it was Murray who consolidated the gains won by Lewis."

John L. Lewis knew that Philip Murray was worth far more to the miners than his $9,000-a-year salary. He once said that Phil knew more about the coal business than $100,000-a-year executives and that none could compare with him in logical argument. When the fiery Lewis knocked "Big Bill" Hutcheson of the Carpenters' Union to the floor of the American Federation of Labor 1935 convention and marched off to form the Committee for Industrial Organization, he took Philip Murray with him. The Committee functioned for a time within the parent trade union organization, despite the opposition of some old-time AFL members. But the differences between the trade union and the industrial union groups multiplied, and soon the AFL expelled the Committee. Then it reorganized as the independent Congress of Industrial Organizations, with John L. Lewis as its first president and Philip Murray as vice president, as mentioned above.

In addition to his work in the steel industry, Murray took an active part in unionizing the electrical, rubber, ship, textile, and auto industries. In 1940, when John L. Lewis resigned, he was elected president of the CIO. His tenure of office, which lasted until his death at sixty-six on November 9, 1952, was marked by common sense and the spirit of compromise, for the virtues he had learned as a negotiator—moderation, patience, conciliation—stood him in good stead in holding together the forty-odd autonomous unions and five million rank and file members of the CIO.

These same characteristics had won him the respect and admiration of leading industrialists also. At his death he was as warmly praised by the men who had battled against him from the other side of the arbitration table as by the workers in mine and factory who had profited directly from his efforts and who remembered him affectionately as Uncle Phil.

As a labor leader, he was tough, knowledgeable, efficient. As a man, he was unassuming, kind, "one of the gentlest of men." He could swap yarns with President Roosevelt and still feel at home later, talking around an iron stove with some of his coal miner friends. Though he was top man in the CIO, there was no intercom on his desk: if he needed someone, he would heave himself out of his chair and walk to the other man's office.

Shocked by his death, the labor movement quickly established a "living memorial" to "encourage and strengthen the values that Phil Murray symbolized." A sum of one million dollars was collected and then disbursed in his name to schools, religious organizations, hospitals, the National Association for the Advancement of Colored People, the American Arbitration Association, the American Association for the United Nations, and the Israeli Federation of Labor.

Igor Sikorsky

MORE than a thousand years ago somewhere in China an unknown artisan, obsessed with the fanciful notion of making a heavy object rise into the thin air, invented the Chinese top. The toy, a marvelous gadget, was lifted high above the earth when its whirling propeller was set in motion by a shaft that the operator spun between the palms of his hands. This toy was the world's first flying machine.

Hundreds of years later Leonardo da Vinci, the famous Italian painter and inventor, rediscovered the principle underlying the Chinese top and designed a spiral air screw capable of rising into the air. The principle, of course, was that of the helicopter, a machine that takes its name from two Greek words: *helix,* meaning "spiral," and *pteron,* meaning "wing."

Other attempts to conquer space through the use of a device that would bite into the air and pull a heavy body upward followed. Small models using bird feathers and springs were developed and flown. In the 1870's a successful seven-pound steam-driven machine incorporating the principle of Da Vinci's air screw took to the air. Several attempts were even made at building a machine large enough to bear a man aloft. But all of these attempts failed.

Few people knew about these curious experiments. Few knew that Da Vinci had ever done anything but paint his wonderful pictures. Or, if they knew, they didn't care, for the man's paintings were so important that, by comparison, anything else he might have accomplished paled to insignificance. But late in the nineteenth century the wife of a university professor in the Russian city of Kiev became interested in Da Vinci. She studied the painter's notebooks, fascinated by his wonderfully fertile mind. And by the time her youngest son, who was born in 1889, reached the tell-me-a-story age, she was so full of the exciting notebooks that she began to amuse her boy by talking about Da Vinci instead of telling him about the imaginary creatures in the Russian fairy tales. The boy, whose name was Igor Ivan Sikorsky, remembered the strange things his mother told him, particularly those concerning Da Vinci's spiral screw. He remembered so well, in fact, that by the time he was twelve years old he had constructed a small helicopter himself. Powered by rubber bands, the little machine actually flew!

As young Igor grew up he continued his experiments in mechanics. He was primarily interested in flying machines, but he tinkered with all sorts of gadgets in the little home workshop behind the house in Kiev. As a matter of fact, when he was but thirteen years old, he constructed a small bomb which he detonated in the back yard. A crew of workmen on a nearby building project stopped to watch the boy. Later they described what they had seen to the contractor on the job, who, in turn, told Igor's father. Professor Sikorsky listened attentively to what he was told, thanked his informant, and returned home. But instead of scolding his son, he praised him for his experiments and told him to continue with them. Igor, encouraged by his understanding father, spent more and more time in the little workshop, eventually producing there such complex contrivances as a steam-driven motorcycle.

At school Igor was a good student, and he was accepted for enrollment in the St. Petersburg Naval College in 1903. Graduating from the college in 1906, he refused the offer of a commission in the Navy and returned to Kiev. There he entered the Polytechnic Institute, bent on becoming an engineer. But he soon discovered that the theory of mechanics was not nearly so exciting as was tinkering with machines. And as there was no tinkering and much theorizing at the institute, Igor became bored and left without taking his degree. Perhaps news about the famous American experiments of the Wright brothers, who had made their first successful airplane flight in 1903, or about the early dirigible flights of Count Zeppelin, had hastened his decision to quit the stuffy Institute. At any rate, he was soon on his way to Paris, then the European center for aeronautical experimentation, to learn all he could about the practical business of building aircraft.

In Paris young Sikorsky discovered that building aircraft was far from being a practical venture. In 1909 the man who went high enough to "break wood," that is, to have a crash, was a creature to be regarded with awe and respect. When Igor asked a French aviator to name the best aircraft engine, he was told, "They are all bad!"

Intent upon acquiring the components of a plane, Igor persisted. "Which is least bad?" he asked.

"The one with the smallest number of parts," was the answer, "for the parts are all bad, too."

Another piece of advice that Igor picked up in Paris was more helpful, and he has always remembered it. Drawn into conversation with a Captain Ferber there, he described his own early experiments in airplane design, perhaps bragging a bit. The Captain eyed him briefly, smiled, and replied concisely, "To invent a flying machine is nothing; to build it is little; to make it fly is everything."

Igor returned to Kiev somewhat chastened. But his spirit was not completely depressed, for he had purchased, despite the warning of his pessimistic aviator friend, a three-cylinder, 25-horsepower Anzani engine. And when he got back to his workshop, he started to build a helicopter to use it in, financed in the work by his sister Olga. Of course, when the craft was completed it did not fly. But Igor was still not depressed. Far from it. He was exuberant, for when he attached his machine to a scale and raced the engine he discovered that it lifted 375 pounds—only 100 pounds less than the weight of the machine!

A second attempt at building a helicopter proved no more successful than the first, and Igor turned his attention to the sort of aircraft that was then establishing itself as the conventional type. But his airplane was as much of a failure as his helicopter. And when a second airplane that he built failed to leave the ground, people began to call him a crackpot and to snicker at his crazy ideas. Nevertheless, some of his friends had faith in him, and with the aid of two or three student engineers with whom he had studied at the institute, and a plumber and two carpenters who were interested in his experiments, he rebuilt his plane, which he called the S-2. Finally, he met with success. On June 3, 1910, after days of taxiing in the neighboring fields the S-2 took to the air. It soared four feet above the ground for twelve seconds, traveling almost 200 yards while aloft! Before the end of the month Sikorsky had piled up almost eight minutes of flying time in his wonderful machine. Then, on June 30, he climbed eighty feet above the earth in the plane and attempted a turn. The machine stalled, hung sickeningly in the air for a moment and plummeted to the ground like a stricken bird. The S-2 was completely demolished, and Sikorsky was almost killed. But he survived the crash, and when he recovered he went back to work on another plane.

Igor's father, who had always been interested in his son's work, was impressed by the boy's accomplishment and by his persistence in the face of discouragement. Now he decided to help the boy by providing him with as much capital as he could spare. Thus, aided by his father as well as by his sister, Igor continued his aeronautical experiments, eventually producing the S-5. On its first flight this machine climbed to an altitude of 300 feet and, after staying in the air for four minutes, made a perfect landing. By 1911 Igor had reached 1,000 feet in the S-5, remaining aloft for a half hour. He had also obtained a pilot's license from the Imperial Aeronautical Club of Russia and had been presented to the Czar after participating in the maneuvers of the Russian Army with his plane. And in the same year the young aviator set a world record, flying the S-5 at the then terrifying speed of 75 m.p.h. while carrying three passengers.

It was while flying the S-5 that Igor Sikorsky got the idea that was to establish him as one of the foremost designers of multi-engine aircraft. And the idea was spawned by a mosquito! One of those pestiferous insects got into the gasoline line of the S-5 and was drawn into the carburetor, stalling the machine and necessitating a forced landing. Sikorsky reasoned that a plane with more than one engine would have been capable of continued flight if such an accident had incapacitated one source of power. In addition, of course, the plane would have added power in normal flight, making it capable of carrying greater loads at higher speeds. Designing such a plane, he won the highest award at the Moscow Aircraft Exhibition of 1912. He also won a contract with the Russo-Baltic Railroad Car Works, as chief designer for their aircraft division. The contract contained a provision which specified that Sikorsky could build one experimental plane a year at company expense. At last he had adequate financial backing for large-scale experimentation. And his salary enabled him to pay back the money his family had contributed to his work. By this time the sum was more than $25,000.

Sikorsky's first experimental plane for the Russo-Baltic Car Works was called the *Grand*. It weighed 9,000 pounds, had a 92-foot wingspan, and was the first four-motor dual-control airplane ever built. In it Sikorsky established another world record in 1913 by staying aloft for one hour and fifty-four minutes with eight passengers aboard.

The Russian airplane builder was soon at work on another plane. When he had completed it in 1914, accompanied by two co-pilots and a mechanic he took it on a 1,500 mile flight from St. Petersburg to Kiev and back. One bit of excitement broke the monotony of the epic flight. Indeed, it almost ended the trip, the plane, and its occupants' lives. A fire suddenly broke out in the big plane as it sped over the bleak Russian steppes. It flared brightly, dangerously close to the fuel supply. Quickly, Sikorsky stripped off the heavy overcoat he was wearing as protection against the biting cold. He fell on the fire with it and, the other members of his crew following suit, the flames were soon extinguished, allowing them to complete the trip without further incident.

During World War I, Sikorsky built military aircraft for the Russian government. A bomber version of his multi-engine plane was the first aircraft to carry and drop thousand-pound bombs on enemy troops and installations. Later in the war Sikorsky added defensive armament to his 17,000-pound bomber. With eleven strategically placed machine guns jutting from apertures in the plane, it seemed to contemporaries that it bristled with guns. In all, Sikorsky supplied 74 bombers to the Russian Army, selling them to the government at $125,-000 each. By the end of the war he was a wealthy man, leaving over $500,000 in bonds and real estate when he fled the country at the outbreak of the Russian Revolution.

Like many Russian émigrés at the time of the Revolution, Sikorsky took refuge in Paris. After a brief stay he moved on to London. Then, in March of 1919, he came to America. Possessing only $600 when he arrived in this country, the famous plane designer immediately sought work in the aircraft industry. But in post-war America there was no aircraft industry, or next to none, for a business slump had reduced airplane production to

a bare minimum. Without work, Sikorsky was soon reduced to a diet of bread and beans. A part-time job in a
settlement house on New York's East Side, where he
taught Russian immigrants aviation, mathematics, and
astronomy, earned him from three to ten dollars a week.
It also helped him to learn English. And in the settlement house he met Elizabeth Semion, who was to become his second wife. His first wife, whom he had married in Russia when he was still little more than a boy,
had died before he left his homeland, leaving him with
a young daughter to care for. As the years passed, Elizabeth, whom he married in New York on January 27,
1924, presented him with four fine sons.

Backed by a small loan from a man named W. A.
Barry, Sikorsky had in 1923 begun working on his first
American plane. Construction was started in an abandoned chicken coop on a farm near Roosevelt Field,
Long Island, a group of Russian friends working without pay to help the designer. Sometimes it was so cold in
the makeshift workshop that the men's fingers froze to
the metal they were working with. But even though
they used second-hand materials and made their own
tools, the devoted group soon exhausted their funds.
Then Sergei Rachmaninoff, the musician, was induced
to invest $5,000 in return for a vice-presidency in the
newly organized Sikorsky Aeronautical Engineering
Corporation. The money enabled the men to rent a
hangar and complete their work on the two-engine

plane. In May 1924, the S-29, as it was called, took off on its test flight. Eight men who had worked on the plane crowded aboard, anxious to participate in its first flight. The overloaded plane lurched across the field and staggered into the air, but the strain was too much for its second-hand motors. They sputtered, coughed, died; and the plane came crashing down in an empty field.

The S-29 was badly damaged, but it was not completely demolished. Sikorsky knew that it could be rebuilt and made to fly if he had a little more money. But there was no more money—unless! He called a hurried meeting of the stockholders of the small corporation. When the stockholders had all assembled, Sikorsky locked the door of the meeting room, pocketed the key, and sat down. He was determined to rebuild his plane, and unless the stockholders provided the capital needed for the completion of the job, he wasn't going to open that door. Such a procedure was outrageous! Sikorsky was using coercion! He was guilty, actually, of kidnapping! He wasn't going to be allowed to get away with such high-handed methods! But before the door of the meeting room was opened $2,500 had been raised.

The sum proved to be sufficient. Sikorsky went to work on the plane, enlarging it so that it was capable of carrying fourteen passengers at speeds of up to 115 miles per hour. When it was completely rebuilt, Sikorsky chartered it as a passenger and transport plane, making over 200 flights in it.

Having built one of the first successful twin-engine planes in America, Sikorsky won more substantial financial backing. In 1925 with new capital he reorganized his company as the Sikorsky Manufacturing Company. Still experimenting, he next built the first tri-motor plane produced in America. Then he turned to a radically new type of aircraft—the amphibian. His S-38, a two-engine, ten-seat amphibian, was a peculiar-looking aircraft. Its hull, wings, and tail were separate and distinct elements, joined only by struts. Old-time pilots seeing it fly over would shout, "There go the spare parts of a Sikorsky, flying in formation!" But the S-38 was a sturdy workhorse of a plane, and it opened new horizons for the aviation industry. Lindbergh inaugurated airmail service between the United States and Panama with one. And, using thirty S-38's, Pan American Airways pioneered its air-travel system in South America. In addition, the planes, which cost from $20,000 to $150,000, were sold to many wealthy American sportsmen as private flying expanded during the postwar boom in America. In all, Sikorsky sold more than one hundred S-38's, realizing a fortune on them.

The stock-market crash of 1929 that brought ruin to so many American businessmen did not hurt Sikorsky. One month before the crash occurred, he had sold his newly organized Sikorsky Aviation Corporation to United Aircraft. Through the sale it became known as United Aircraft's Vought-Sikorsky Aircraft Division.

The noted designer did not become an executive in the new corporation. Caring little for the financial manipulations characteristic of big business, he chose instead to continue contributing to the practical end of the industry, taking a job as engineering manager of the new division.

It was Sikorsky who designed the $30,000 wind-tunnel for the Vought-Sikorsky plant. And it was Sikorsky, of course, who brought world fame to the company and himself by designing the enormous clippers, or flying boats, that pioneered in establishing regular service over both oceans. The twenty-ton S-42, which Sikorsky built in 1934, was the largest flying boat of its day. Capable of carrying thirty-two passengers and a crew of five, it broke ten world's records for speed, altitude, and pay load, and proved to airplane manufacturers like Martin and Boeing that aircraft could be both large and economical. One particular economy that Sikorsky's research was responsible for was the reduction of the wingspan of large aircraft with a consequent increase of wing load, or amount of weight borne by each square foot of wing. Ridiculing the idea that a light wing load was essential to safety, the Russian-born designer observed: "The albatross rides the storm with perfect ease, but just see what happens to the butterfly with its light wing load. It is blown away."

Having built some of the world's largest aircraft with relatively short wings, Sikorsky now decided to build small craft with no wings at all! He still remembered his mother's talks about Da Vinci's spiral air screw. And he determined to build a helicopter, despite his early failures with the type. Interest in craft of this sort had been revived by the invention of the autogiro, the first practical departure from the fixed wing airplane. But the autogiro, a compromise between an airplane and a true helicopter, was little more than an aerial curiosity. It could not ascend vertically, for its free-spinning wind-mill-like rotor was unpowered. The engine merely drove a conventional propeller that provided forward motion, causing the rotor to revolve and lift the plane into the air. Sikorsky decided to build a true helicopter. And after years of research and an outlay of $300,000, on September 14, 1939, his experiments reached fruition. On that day the V-S 300, a wingless framework of welded iron pipe equipped with a 75-horsepower engine, was lifted vertically into the air by its single whirling rotor. A new era in aviation history had begun.

There was, however, some delay in getting started. On its first flight the VS-300 had risen only a few inches from the ground. It was not until the spring of 1940 that Sikorsky took the machine up for its first sustained flight. It did *almost* everything he wanted it to do. It ascended and descended vertically. It hovered motionless in mid-air. It flew to the right and the left. It even flew backward. There was only one thing it would not do. It would not fly forward! Spectators laughed derisively, calling the helicopter "Igor's folly." Soon, though, they were of a different mind. Before Pearl Harbor Sikorsky had ironed out all of the "bugs" in his 'copter. During the war it was used extensively for liaison, reconnaissance, and aerial rescue work. By the time of the Korean conflict the helicopter had developed tremendously, and the "eggbeater," as the UN troops called it, proved an invaluable asset in the mountainous and swampy terrain of Korea. Over one thousand crashed pilots were rescued from behind enemy lines by the little "whirlybirds." Twenty thousand casualties were evacuated by 'copter. In addition, the helicopter laid mines; hauled troops, weapons, and supplies; strung wire; reconnoitered, and did a thousand and one military jobs.

The Vietnam War saw a much greater use of the helicopter, as well as further technical refinements. The quick evacuation of the wounded from battlefields by helicopters reduced the number of soldiers who died from head or abdominal wounds from 80 per cent to 10 per cent.

In nonmilitary work it has been used for mail and passenger service, for rescue and police work, for short-haul freight and aerial photography. Rooftop landing spaces are used commercially in cities to provide fast shuttle service between the cities and outlying airports. The Coast Guard now has Sikorsky helicopters that can land on water, making rescues at sea much easier.

In 1965, a Sikorsky helicopter achieved the record

speed of 242 miles an hour. In that same year, another of his helicopters completed the first transatlantic flight.

In the early sixties, Sikorsky and his men developed and built what they called the flying crane—a helicopter made up of a front-end cab for the pilot and a long, high backbone. Cargo of any type or shape can be fitted under this backbone. Entire battlefield "hospitals" have been airlifted in Vietnam by the "sky crane," as have communication shacks.

Sikorsky envisions the sky crane as the cargo workhorse of the future. When three-hour jet flights between London and New York become a commonplace, passengers will not want to spend two hours at the beginning and end of their trips fighting ground traffic between city and airport. Sikorsky sees the sky crane as the ten-minute answer. Passengers will step from their jet into a cabin, which will be picked up by a flying crane and deposited on a rooftop in the center of town in ten minutes.

Sikorsky also suggested that the sky crane could eliminate the need for long runways in heavily congested urban areas. A jetliner on a skyscraper rooftop would be lifted by the flying crane and accelerated until the jet could fly by itself. At the destination city, the jet would slow down. A waiting sky crane would rendezvous with it, catch it midair, slow it down further and set it gently on another rooftop—much as a tugboat helps an ocean liner to dock.

Another use of the crane would create an entirely new mass production housing industry! Sikorsky said it would be possible to manufacture complete homes in an assembly-line factory, pick up the homes with sky cranes and fly them to sites. The crane would place the home on the foundation. He said that $25,000 homes could thus be sold for $10,000.

As Igor Sikorsky once told a group of senators, "The book of literally unlimited possibilities for the helicopter has only been opened and the nation will have no reason to regret every effort that has been made" to bring the helicopter into wide use.

David Dubinsky

THE police captain looked sourly at the sixty-odd men. They were milling about in the big room that served as an emergency prison cell in the city jail of Lodz in Russian Poland. A weird bunch, thought the captain. They were all Jewish, they were all bakers, they were all crazy unionists and they were all strikers. In 1907, under Czarist law, workers could belong to trade unions, as long as they weren't political groups. But it was a crime to strike.

One of the prisoners was a young lad dressed in an Orthodox Jewish ceremonial robe. His father had thrust the robe on him in an effort to save him at the moment of arrest. He was a short fellow, with bushy hair and a bright, impudent face. The captain judged him to be no more than twelve or thirteen, yet he was jabbering quietly in one corner with a group of grown men as though he were their equal, or even, perhaps, their leader.

Curious about the youngster's role in the strike, the captain walked over to him and learned that his name was David Dobnievski, that he was actually fifteen years old despite his small size and that he had been a master baker for the past year.

When he asked the lad what he was doing among the "lawbreakers" in the room, David replied, "I'm here with them because I believe in their fight for a living wage and because I'm secretary of their union. We went on strike because we think working ninety hours a week for small pay is sheer slavery."

The captain looked at the young man for a moment and then asked, "Where do you live, David?"

"16 Vschodnia Street."

"And your father, is he head of your union?"

"No, he owns a bakery at 16 Vschodnia Street."

"And you helped organize a strike against your own father?" the captain asked incredulously.

"Certainly, but his was only one of the many bakeries we struck."

"What did your father say about his ungrateful son?"

"He gave me his blessing before I came down here," David said quietly, and then smiled at the captain's astonished expression.

David Dobnievski would in a few years simplify his name to Dubinsky, a name adopted by his older brother, who had preceded him to America. He would change his trade, and, in time, become the leader of one of the richest, biggest, and most powerful trade unions in the United States, the International Ladies Garment Work-

ers Union. He would free the Jewish and Italian needle
workers from the vestiges of the sweatshop in New
York and other cities in America. He would fight
against union racketeering in the American labor movement. He would become an implacable foe of communism. He would endow the union movement with a
great sense of social responsibility. He would help create
two new political parties. When Dubinsky retired in
June of 1966 at the age of seventy-four, after serving almost thirty-four years as president of the ILGWU,
George Meany, head of the AFL-CIO, said of him: "No
one, I suppose, will ever completely tabulate all the good
that David Dubinsky achieved in his lifetime."

David Dubinsky was born in Brest-Litovsk in Russian
Poland, on February 22, 1892, the youngest of nine chil-
dren. When David was only two, the family moved to
Lodz.

Lodz was Poland's second largest city, with a half-
million people. It was an ugly, dirty, slum-ridden place,
Poland's most industrialized urban center. Electric trol-
ley cars carried its workers to the factories, but if cheap
transportation was considered a necessity, sanitation
wasn't. Lodz had no sewage system. Raw sewage and
factory wastes flowed down the gutters of even its main
streets. Millionaires lived in mansions right next to their
factories and on the other side of the mansions lived the
workers in their slums. The workers labored up to fifteen hours a day, six days a week. The manufacturers

had the help of Cossacks, the Czar's specially trained soldiers, to keep the men from striking.

David's father was but one of scores of poor Jews who came to Lodz, hoping to make some money by opening small stores. Many started out with a barrel of pickles, some herring, and soda water. David's father, a very religious, sad-eyed, white-bearded man, brought his family to a basement apartment at 16 Vschodnia Street and opened a bakery.

Vschodnia Street was narrow and crowded, with crooked sidewalks and rows of three- and four-story tenements. David's new home consisted of a small front room, a kitchen, a back bedroom, and a middle room with a big oven in it. In the summer, David slept in the delivery wagon in the yard. In the winter, he slept in the kitchen, where the bakers, working at night, put fresh bread to cool on large boards at the head of his bed.

David was luckier than most of the other children on Vschodnia Street. He studied Hebrew and Yiddish in a Zionist school and attended a public school where he learned to read and write in Polish, Russian, and German and became skilled in arithmetic. Frequently punished for unruly behavior, and sent to the school's detention room, he often left that room in a shambles, for which he was further punished. Once a week, he used to go to a dusty yard on Cegielniana Street where he paid a man a few kopecks for the privilege of riding a rented bicycle round and round in the yard for half an hour.

At thirteen his schooling ended abruptly, because he was needed in his father's bakery. He learned baking skills quickly and soon became a "master baker." Meanwhile, he attended meetings of the "Bund"—the General Jewish Workers Union, a revolutionary group agitating for better social conditions.

The Bund, after organizing illegal strikes in other cities, had been forced to operate secretly. Finally, the Bund came to Lodz and formed, among other unions, a bakers' union. David joined and was immediately elected assistant secretary because he was good at figures and was one of the few members who could read and write. Soon after, he was elected secretary.

The union's first big project was the strike for higher wages against all of Lodz's Jewish bakeries, including the one owned by David's father. For his part in the strike, David was kept in jail for ten days. He would have stayed there longer, but his father paid the police captain a bribe of twenty-five rubles. David was released on condition that he leave town immediately.

In later years, Dubinsky recalled what happened next. "An uncle of mine, Moshe Wishingrad, lived in Brest-Litovsk," he said, "so I went there and stayed with him for three months, doing nothing. Then I got sick and tired of it and I returned to Lodz without permission of the police." He rejoined his union comrades and started baking again, jumping from bakery to bakery to stay out of sight of the police.

David was caught on January 8, 1908, at a meeting of the union. The police had issued a permit for the meeting, but only in order to trap the men. After weeks of unexplained imprisonment, David was finally interrogated by the chief of police, led out of jail under guard and marched off to Siberia to live in a small village under police surveillance.

It took eighteen months to transport David to his place of exile. Under Cossack or police guard, he stayed in several jails on the way, usually in the company of thieves, burglars, and even a few murderers. They all liked young Dubinsky and treated him warmly as a "political." Politicals, they felt, sacrificed their whole lives and futures for "everybody."

David also met fellow politicals in the prison—Jewish socialists from the Bund, Polish social-democrats, Russian socialists and members of other organizations. He read the books that were smuggled in and out, and learned how to distinguish one revolutionary group and its goals from those of another. He engaged in long and heated discussions on what the future society should be like. The prisoners slept on the bare floor, after pouring circles of water around themselves to keep the bedbugs away.

Following a long stay in a prison in Samara, David and some of his friends were loaded onto a train that took them to Chelyabinsk in Siberia. There he learned that his new home would be a village hundreds of miles away and that he would journey to it by foot. The prisoners marched from eight in the morning to six at night, covering twenty to thirty miles a day, with nothing to eat but black bread and hot water.

After six days of this, David made up his mind to escape. As he recalled it years later:

> The most prominent man among the criminals was one Krynin, a strong, hardened man and very taciturn. The other criminals always followed his lead. Early in the morning, I gave Krynin my extra clothes, keeping only those I was wearing. I didn't ask him for any money and I didn't tell him why I was giving him the clothes. As a matter of fact, neither he nor I said a word. But he understood.
>
> The moment the guards sat down to breakfast, I quietly walked out. I went slowly, without looking back. It is perfectly possible that the guards saw me go out and guessed my purpose. As I learned later, they weren't too eager to capture escaped prisoners. They received nine kopeks a day—five cents—for the rations for each of their charges; when a prisoner died en route or escaped, they managed to keep this money for themselves.

By his wits, by some good luck, and by befriending peasants along his escape route, David managed to find his way back to Chelyabinsk where other exiles hid him for six months. He finally made contact with his father, who sent him twenty-five rubles. David then made his way back to Lodz under an assumed name and took odd baking jobs. He changed his sleeping place almost every night to escape discovery by the police. A few months later, an older brother in New York sent him a steamship ticket to America, and late in the fall of 1910, he was smuggled across the German border. From there, it was easy to get to Antwerp, where he boarded a ship for the heralded land of freedom and opportunity. He arrived in New York Harbor on January 1, 1911. He was not quite nineteen when he began a new life.

David's older brother lived with his family on Clinton Street near East Broadway on New York's bustling Lower East Side. After his reunion with his brother, David announced, "I'm through with baking. I will learn a new trade in this new land, and I will earn some money at once, so I won't be a burden to you."

He had worked only a few weeks as a dishwasher and as a maker of "knee pants," when he decided to learn cloak-cutting, one of the highest paid crafts in the garment trade.

The cloak cutters were highly skilled—they had to be—for one wrong slice of the knife could ruin a great deal of cloth. After passing a tough test given by the union's examiners, David received his first membership card in the Cutters Union, Local 10, of the International Ladies Garment Workers Union, on July 13, 1911.

The ILGWU was only eleven years old when Dubinsky became a member. It had its roots in the huge immigration of Jews from eastern Europe that began in the 1880's and continued unabated until the outbreak of

World War I in 1914. At its peak, Jewish immigration averaged one hundred thousand a year. Great numbers of Jews went into the needle trades in New York and other big cities, both as manufacturers and as workers. Small entrepreneurs used their homes as workshops, hiring new arrivals as they came, and the "sweatshop" was born, with all its evils of overcrowding, long hours, low pay, lack of sanitation, light and air.

A host of small garment unions grew out of the constant arguments between employers and employees. The workers felt they could present their complaints better to their bosses if they banded together in unions. So, every work season started with strikes by the workers. Agreements on wages would be made. But then, these agreements were broken by the employers toward the end of the season when work was scarce.

The unions never lasted long. The industry was too fluid, with manufacturers springing up overnight and going bankrupt soon afterward, leaving workers stranded without jobs. The industry was afflicted by changing styles, depressions and recessions and a high turnover of workers. The unions were split among themselves by factional battles between anarchists and socialists of various shades.

Finally, the need for a larger, and hopefully more effective union of garment unions became apparent. In 1900 the ILGWU was founded by a few locals which together had a total of about two thousand members. By the time Dubinsky became a member of the powerful Cutters Local eleven years later, the ILGWU was a relatively strong organization of some seventy-five thousand members with permanent recognition by the manufacturers.

It was not until five years after he had joined that Dubinsky became actively involved in union affairs. In the beginning he did not know English, and he was much more interested in socialism and its ideals than in unionism for its own sake. He had joined the Socialist Party soon after his arrival.

In those days it was a very common thing for men with strong political, social, or religious convictions to stand on street corners and in parks, lecturing the passing crowds and trying to interest them in their ideas. Dubinsky ran into several dedicated socialists who had been fellow Bund members in Europe and were now speakers of this sort. The young cutter joined them. After a hard day's work in the cutting room, he would follow his friends from corner to corner, lugging soapboxes for them. Once in a while, he introduced them. Soon, he was making speeches himself in Yiddish, haranguing whatever crowd he could gather and snapping answers back at hecklers.

In 1914 at the age of twenty-two, he met Emma Goldberg. Emma, in the words of one person who knew her, was "an attractive, vivacious, slim brunette, with a sustained zest for the things which make life fuller." She was also a member of the ILGWU. Like David, she was an immigrant, having come from Czarist Lithuania. Dubinsky fell in love with her and married her.

Dubinsky eventually tired of speechmaking. He was at heart a very practical young man. It was fun arguing theories, but for him theory had to result in some kind of action.

He finally threw himself wholeheartedly into union work during the cloakmakers' strike of 1916, picketing, helping out at strike headquarters, aiding the strikers in small, personal ways. He found his place in Local 10 and, characteristically, worked like a demon. Although he was still a socialist, Dubinsky felt that the important thing was finding what was best for the union and then acting to get it. Many years later, questioned about his early blasts against "capitalistic society," Dubinsky responded, "Unions need capitalism like a fish needs water."

In 1918 he was elected a member of the executive board of Local 10; in 1920 the local's vice president; in 1921, president; and soon after, general manager of the local. Dubinsky stepped onto the national scene in 1922, when he was elected a vice-president and a member of the ILGWU's General Executive Board at the union's convention in Cleveland. At the time, the ILGWU had 115,000 members throughout the United States and Canada.

The influence of the Communist Party on the labor

movement has been exaggerated. Nonetheless, Communists did gain power in some unions, and by 1924 they had taken control of the three largest locals of the ILGWU. They were elected as the majority faction on the executive boards of Locals 2, 9, and 22 in New York City. The Union's national body, the General Executive Board, suspended the three locals, which then formed a Joint Action Committee. The JAC began operating as a dual union among the garment workers—it collected dues, handled shop grievances, and pressed employers for recognition.

In July 1926, the Joint Board, under JAC domination, called a general strike that involved 50,000 workers in New York City. It lasted twenty-seven weeks, ending in January 1927, with a serious loss by the workers of many of their previously hard-won rights. It was a disaster, financially, costing about $3,500,000 and leaving the union with a $2,000,000 debt. Although the strike was inspired by the suspended locals, the national organization assumed the costs of the strike once the general walkout began.

During all this conflict, the Communists were never able to establish a beachhead in Local 10, of which Dubinsky had remained the general manager even though he was a vice-president of the national body. Dubinsky watched and ruled his local with a one-man control, cultivating those who were loyal to him, undercutting any moves to infiltrate the local. When the strike was over,

Local 10 emerged as the strongest unit of the ILGWU and the only local that was not in debt.

During the strike, Dubinsky was threatened several times with bodily harm. "Get a gun permit and carry a gun," his friends advised him repeatedly. "Why should I get a gun, I'm not afraid of them," he would say. He finally listened to the advice, but admitted later that since he was the slowest draw in the East, he kept the gun in an office desk drawer and carried it only on his way home if he left a strike meeting after midnight.

When the strike ended, Dubinsky and the other national officers succeeded in ousting Communists from power positions in New York, Chicago, Boston, Philadelphia, Montreal, Baltimore, and San Francisco. But the strike had left the union weak. Membership fell; garment workers were suspicious after the debacle. Once burned, twice cautious was the general attitude when union organizers tried to lure the workers back into the fold. Manufacturers took constant advantage of the union's small membership and, hence, lack of real power. Bosses could arbitrarily fire anyone who belonged to the union, since unions had no legal recognition.

Dubinsky played an active part in peddling union "reconstruction" bonds during 1927, '28 and '29, but the debts were hard to pay off.

Came the October 1929 crash on Wall Street, and the union faced a bleak future, with the country on the threshold of the Great Depression of the thirties. In December 1929, Dubinsky was persuaded to resign as general manager of Local 10 and take on the full-time job of secretary-treasurer of the ILGWU. With his uncanny ability to make a union dollar stretch as far as it could be stretched, Dubinsky was able to reduce the ILGWU debt by one million dollars during the next three years.

Still, it was a very shaky union when Dubinsky took over as ILGWU president in 1932, at the age of forty. Many observers predicted that Dubinsky would be the union's last president; they did not give the union much more time to live.

The new ILGWU president had to walk up and down the stairs at union headquarters, because the elevator had been shut down. There was no money to pay the electric bill. The union staff was unpaid. ILGWU membership at the time stood at a low of forty thousand. What was left of the union was still torn by internal quarreling. Even though Dubinsky's financial wizardry had reduced the union's debt, there was still another million to pay back. The Great Depression was on. People selling apples on street corners and standing in bread lines would soon be a common sight. The garment industry was chaotic, and with work scarce, the ILGWU didn't stand much of a chance to organize the demoralized workers.

When Dubinsky took over as president in June of

1932, the New York cloakmakers were preparing for a strike. But neither the manufacturers nor Dubinsky was ready for a fight to the finish. The final settlement called for a ten per cent wage scale reduction—a bitter pill for the new president to swallow.

In November, New York's Governor Franklin D. Roosevelt was elected President of the United States. One of Roosevelt's major attacks on the depression was the National Industrial Recovery Act (NRA), which was passed in July 1933. The NRA gave labor the legal right to organize into unions. It set employment standards for each industry, fixed minimum wage scales, and to spread the available work reduced working hours in virtually all industries to forty a week. The ILGWU managed to get working hours for its own members reduced to thirty-five a week. The shops and plants that met the NRA's requirements displayed signs and labels which had the NRA "blue eagle" on them.

Dubinsky saw the NRA's value to his union when it was first introduced in Congress. It gave unions the long-sought-for legal right to organize workers. Weeks before it was passed, he started feverish organization drives in almost sixty cities. A month after NRA passed New York dressmakers tied up their industry with a strike, and city mediators stepped in to bring the factory owners and Dubinsky together. New York *Journal-American* editor Arthur Brisbane described Dubinsky's part in the negotiations this way:

"It was a delight to watch and to hear David Dubinsky, head of the ILG, as he took the floor, beginning always mildly, ending otherwise with 'We don't want to wait to eat pie-in-the-sky' . . . . His spine is bent at the top, from years of working over machines, turning out garments that others wear. But when he rises, shakes his small hand, with soft, round fingers, although he is only five feet four, he looks like a giant . . . ."

To the men and women in his union, Dubinsky *was* a giant. Impudent in his youth, he was now a brash, flamboyant, rough-and-tumble, sentimental labor leader whose sole passion was his union. Many years later, A. H. Raskin, the labor expert of *The New York Times,* called him a "volcanic man" with "a voice that starts as a shout and works up the decibel scale from there."

Raskin went on to describe how he "takes tickets at union functions, adjusts the microphones, peels off his dinner jacket to help the waiters set up extra banquet tables, quarrels over the price of floor tile and switches off the light in empty union offices, leaving behind a note with some such reproof as 'What's the matter, Edison gives it to you free?' "

Led by Dubinsky, and with the new NRA on their side, the New York dressmakers won their August strike, gaining a thirty-five-hour week, a closed union shop, which forbade employers to hire anyone unless he or she was a union member, job security and other fringe benefits. Dubinsky went on to further organization victories in other parts of the garment industry throughout the country. In 1935 the United States Supreme Court declared the NRA unconstitutional, but Dubinsky and the ILGWU had become so powerful in three years that they lost none of the gains they had won under the NRA. Membership was up to 200,000, all debts had been paid, and the union had assets of $850,000.

In October 1934, Dubinsky had been elected a vice-president of the American Federation of Labor (AFL) and the ILGWU's influence on the national labor scene was greatly enhanced. At the time, there was a group within the American labor movement that wanted to organize the mass production industries along the lines of "industrial unionism."

This differed from the way most AFL unions were organized; namely, along the lines of "craft unionism." A "craft" union is usually made up of one kind of worker in many industries. An "industrial" union takes in many kinds of workers in a single industry. Thus, a union made up of bakers whose members worked in hotels, restaurants, small bakeshops, and large baking plants would be a craft union. A union of clerks, cleaners, telephone operators, guards, and assembly-line men who worked only in automobile factories would be an industrial union.

John L. Lewis, president of the United Mine Workers, was the leader of the movement for industrial unions. He wanted the AFL to change its policies to permit this new way of organizing mass production workers. Dubinsky sided with Lewis.

At the 1935 AFL convention in Atlantic City, the festering issue came to a head. Opponents of industrial unionism foresaw too much overlapping of "jurisdictions," that is, a group of workers in a certain craft might also be part of a larger group of workers in a single industry. Few leaders of craft unions were willing to reorganize; they felt uncertain about what they might gain by giving up part of their jurisdictions—they were comfortable with the status quo.

The convention refused to approve industrial unionism, and after it was over, Lewis formed a Committee for Industrial Organization to write a dissenting minority report. Lewis had Dubinsky and the ILGWU on his side, as well as the hatters' union, the textile workers, and the oil field workers. Dubinsky never intended the committee to establish itself as a rival federation. He had thought the committee would work for its goals within the AFL. But Lewis resigned from the AFL and started an organizing campaign among steel workers.

The following year, Dubinsky found it impossible to keep his dual position as an officer of the AFL and as a sympathizer with Lewis. So he resigned from the vice-presidency. Nevertheless, for two years, he tried to mediate the conflict between Lewis and the AFL leaders.

Dubinsky soon found that Lewis was impossible to work with. Lewis did many things which Dubinsky found objectionable. When Lewis started to take Communists and radicals into the committee, he brushed aside Dubinsky's protests with the explanation that he was only using them. "Who gets the bird, David, the hunter or the dog?" Lewis asked.

When later Lewis found himself attacked by the Communists, he admitted that Dubinsky had been right. Dubinsky couldn't resist the impulse to needle Lewis and he asked, "Who was the hunter, John, and who was the dog?"

It finally dawned on Dubinsky that no peace could be achieved between Lewis and the AFL. When Dubinsky saw in 1938 that Lewis really meant to establish a rival organization of unions, he resigned from the committee. Shortly after his resignation, the committee became the Congress of Industrial Organizations (CIO) and the jurisdictional wars between the AFL and the CIO began.

Dubinsky kept the ILGWU independent for a year and a half, but he rejoined the AFL in 1940, too much a part of the national union movement to remain unaffiliated. He said, in explaining the move, "We derived our moral and spiritual sustenance from being an integral part of the entire labor movement."

Dubinsky and a dedicated minority within the AFL then worked hard for years to bring about a reconciliation between the two rival labor federations. Finally, in 1955 the groups merged into the AFL-CIO.

In the intervening years, Dubinsky was actively engaged in politics. He had always felt that labor should have a political voice, because much legislation affected the nation's economy, sometimes hurting the working man, sometimes helping him.

As a teen-aged master baker in Lodz, Dubinsky had allied himself with socialism, and suffered imprisonment and exile for his political beliefs. For several years after he came to America, he believed strongly in socialist theories as the answer to society's problems. Active unionism, however, gradually pulled him away from this belief. In 1932 he wholeheartedly embraced the antidepression policies of Franklin Roosevelt. In 1934 after the enactment of the National Recovery Act and others, he resigned from the Socialist Party. In 1936 he and other union leaders formed the American Labor Party.

During World War II, Dubinsky served on various government boards. Meanwhile, the ALP was gradually coming under the influence of political radicals. In 1944 Dubinsky pulled out of the ALP, and with him went the ILGWU's enormous influence and financial backing. Dubinsky and several other liberals then formed the Liberal Party of New York State.

The Liberal Party swiftly developed into an active political organization—with local clubs, precinct captains, election workers, and a line on the voting machine or paper ballot. Most of the time, the Liberals endorsed Democratic candidates, but sometimes they endorsed Republicans and sometimes the Liberals ran their own candidates. Often a candidate from one of the two major parties found that Liberal endorsement provided the margin of victory in New York State for him.

Dubinsky's interest in politics never made him forget that first and foremost he was a labor leader, head of the ILGWU, with a strong stake in the national labor movement.

One of his constant battles was against corruption and racketeering in unions. Some locals, for example, were headed by men who drew up weak contracts for their members in exchange for bribes by employers. The "clean" union leaders knew what was going on, but for the sake of the national labor movement, they said and did nothing. Dubinsky had just rejoined the AFL in 1940 when, always a boat-rocker if he felt he was right, he proposed an anti-rackets program at the AFL convention in New Orleans. For this and several other proposals, he was punched in the nose by Joseph Fay, a leader of the union of operating engineers. Fay was later convicted and jailed for extortion.

Dubinsky's constant agitation for cleaner unions finally resulted in an anti-rackets code for the merged labor movement in 1957. Dubinsky also fought a running battle for antidiscrimination measures, both in politics and in the unions.

As for the ILGWU, when Dubinsky retired, his union had 447,000 members, about 80 per cent of all ladies garment workers—the rest was non-union labor. The ILGWU said good-bye to Dubinsky with 600 million dollars in funds and reserves, including the most complete welfare program for its members in the United States. In his time, Dubinsky had helped to stabilize the ladies' garment industry. After the organizing strikes of the Thirties, there hadn't been a strike in more than a quarter of a century. The ILGWU had built a huge, 20 million dollar co-operative housing project on the lower East Side of New York and a 40 million dollar development in mid-Manhattan; a 1,000-acre vacation resort for its members, Unity House, in the Pocono Mountains of Pennsylvania; model health centers in thirteen cities. It had gone into theater and movie ventures—its most famous production was a musical comedy called *Pins and Needles*. It had given tens of millions of dollars to labor and charitable causes throughout the world; developed its own staff of industrial engineers to help employers; even made loans to a few manufacturers to preserve members' job opportunities; and was a financial angel for a Rockefeller agency, helping to build several housing projects in Puerto Rico.

But for all the job security and fringe benefits that Dubinsky provided for union members, such as longer vacations and larger pensions, they remain on the lower rungs of the nation's wage ladder, and this has been one source of criticism of Dubinsky, both in and out of labor. Their average weekly wage in 1966 was $67.00 per week compared with the national average for soft goods workers of $95.00 The critics say Dubinsky should have put more of his negotiation gains into wages instead of additional fringe benefits. Dubinsky's adherents defend the low wages by saying they have helped to keep an only marginally profitable industry from dropping into chaos.

When Dubinsky announced his retirement, one manufacturer told a *New York Times* reporter: "Dubinsky is one of those union leaders who always expected the manufacturer to make a profit. He knew that as we prospered, the workers would have a continuity of employment and the assurance of better wages . . . . Much as he wanted to see union rates go up, he could not push them up too much above the non-union plants or we would have been put at an even greater cost-price disadvantage."

Perhaps Dubinsky adopted this attitude after remembering the bakers' strike he had helped organize against his own father in Lodz. The workers had won more pay, but his father was one of the bakery owners who was forced out of business as a result of the higher wages. Dubinsky may well have reasoned, what good are higher wages on paper, if you're out of work? In any event, he concentrated on winning for his workers higher pension funds and other fringe benefits, rather than dramatic pay increases.

Dubinsky also came under criticism for refusing to let some of his organizers and business agents, employees of the ILGWU, form their own union to negotiate higher wages with him. Moreover, the National Association for the Advancement of Colored People has accused the ILGWU of discrimination against Negroes and Puerto Ricans. There was criticism when Dubinsky made his son-in-law manager of an ILGWU local, after the young man married Dubinsky's only child.

And some of the ILGWU staff and many manufacturers resented Dubinsky's poppa-knows-best attitude, his complete domination of the union and the industry, and his demands on his members for blind loyalty to him. Once Dubinsky jumped to the top of a table during a summer party at Unity House and shouted jokingly, "Everybody holler, Hurray for Dubinsky!" And everybody did, but some found this kind of joke hard to swallow.

Perhaps it was Dubinsky's early struggles against the Communists that developed in him a wariness of internal arguments. In order to keep factions within the union suppressed, he maintained a one-man control, according to some observers, over all union activities.

His constant battle against racketeers made him demand signed, but undated, resignations of all elected and appointed ILGWU officials—which he kept in his desk. His explanation? "It's conducive to keep your union clean, very conducive." If it was found that an official was engaged in corrupt practices, Dubinsky could "accept the resignation" and say publicly that the man was no longer affiliated with the ILGWU. The critics, of course, saw this as one more way in which Dubinsky was able to maintain an iron-fisted rule over the union.

The ILGWU defends Dubinsky and itself against such criticisms with great vigor. Union spokesmen note that the ILGWU was willing to let its organizers form their own union, but not its business agents, because the business agents helped to make union policy.

The union indignantly denies that it discriminates against Negroes and Puerto Ricans, pointing out that the union is open to all and that Negroes and Puerto Ricans hold jobs on all levels.

On Dubinsky's appointment of the young man who married his daughter, a union spokesman, after noting that this was "an honorable American tradition," said that Dubinsky's son-in-law "had made a distinguished career for himself in the ILGWU in a number of different offices long before entering matrimony."

Dubinsky's paternalism is defended as a "useful technique" which "brought improvements to workers and industry alike." The union denies that Dubinsky exerted one-man rule, saying that "he would reach far out to stimulate an opposition, thereby dramatizing local union election campaigns."

Whatever the defenses, the criticisms were there, and grew. Perhaps Dubinsky was hurt personally by them, for one day in March 1966, he went to a routine meeting of ILGWU officials with a special announcement he had prepared.

The seventy-four-year-old Dubinsky looked at his colleagues and told them he wanted to say something. Tears came to his eyes as they waited.

"In an organization or in human life," he began, "nothing is permanent or forever." He then told them he was stepping down the next month. They were stunned, and then all began talking at the same time, trying to dissuade him.

"No," he said, dabbing the tears from his eyes, "no, it's a decision six months already. I told President Johnson about it on the phone last week and he was a little shocked. It was a tough decision to make, but once I made it, I felt good."

The other union leaders continued to press him. Some embraced him. "Stay on, David," they pleaded. "Change your mind."

Dubinsky replied, "I didn't have a life; I had a union life. I don't want to die in my boots. I'm not waiting for a free funeral. I want to be free."

And when he did formally retire in April, even his critics admitted that, despite his shortcomings, his massive accomplishments made him one of the great leaders of the American labor movement.

Raymond Loewy

"I HAVE always believed," says French-born designer Raymond Loewy, "that society could be industrialized without becoming ugly, and this has been my ruling philosophy." In pursuing his ideal, Loewy has become "the Mr. Big of industrial design." Indeed, he has been credited with the invention of that profession. But, having transformed the appearance of many objects produced by American industry, Loewy is content to let others have the credit for inventing the profession, which, according to him, combines "the functions of the artist, engineer, and silent salesman," making manufactured articles handsome as well as useful. Loewy makes a great deal of money through his own skillful combination of the functions of artist, engineer, and salesman, grossing millions of dollars annually. But despite his tremendous profits, he claims, "It is a poor designer who cannot save his clients more than the fee they pay him." In illustration, he can point to the markedly increased volume of sales of almost every product upon which he has been consulted.

Loewy has been charged with being more concerned

with creating striking designs to encourage an increase in sales than with creating designs of enduring beauty. Critics point out his addiction to streamlined forms, noting that such shapes are appropriate in objects like airplanes, where wind resistance is a significant factor, but inappropriate in the wide variety of products in which Loewy has used them. He defends his idiosyncrasy, asserting that the streamlined form satisfies "a craving for tidiness and simplification" even when it has no practical function. He is aware that sensational designs can be used to disguise the faults of technically shoddy products, but he condemns such practices as unethical. "No reputable member of the profession," he says, "would offer a design that was less sound than he could make it within the limits of cost, available materials, and public taste."

Loewy himself has done a great deal toward overcoming these limits. He has convinced executives that they "must give major consideration to esthetics." The result has been a great increase in industrial budget allotments for design improvement. Indicative of this trend was the Pennsylvania Railroad's allocation of $18,000,000 for a series of experimental locomotives designed by Loewy in 1934. As for materials, Loewy has overcome many of the prejudices formerly governing their choice. His extensive use of plastics, for instance, has helped to popularize them and has resulted in the expansion of the plastics industry. And in defiance of maritime traditions, he has designed all-metal ship interiors, thus reducing fire hazards and insuring liners like the *Panama* and the *Cristobal,* whose staterooms he designed, against the flaming fate of the *Morro Castle.* Even public taste has been radically altered by Loewy, for the simplicity of his designs has encouraged a popular revolt against the inelegant designs with which industry so long flooded the country.

Loewy's concern with good design is no mere part-time or business interest. It is a lifelong preoccupation. As a matter of fact, so deep-seated is his attitude that as a young soldier in World War I he designed and cut his own uniform rather than go into battle in the awkward and ill-fitting general-issue uniform. And his dugout was the best decorated one on the Western Front, being carpeted, draped, and wall-papered with soothing Parisian materials. Despite his concern with clothes and furnishings, however, Loewy's war record in the French Army was outstanding. Trained as an engineer, he was awarded the Croix de Guerre for snaking across no-man's land to plant wires for ground communication within twelve feet of the German trenches. Severely burned in a mustard-gas attack at Reims, Loewy was saved by a young American ambulance driver. Upon his recovery he was made a captain. And by the end of the war he had acquired seven decorations for valor.

Even before the war, Loewy's interest in good design was apparent. In 1906 at the age of thirteen, he won the

J. Gordon Bennett Medal for a model airplane that he designed and built. During the medal competition his plane established a distance record by its one-minute flight in the Bois de Boulogne, near his home in Paris. Previous to winning the Bennett medal, Loewy's interests had been literary. At the age of twelve he had edited and published a magazine, encouraged by his father Maximilian, a Viennese gentleman noted as a writer on finance. However, the boy later decided to become an engineer. When he finished his secondary schooling at Chaptal Collège, in 1910, he enrolled for a course in engineering at L'École de Lanneau. Undoubtedly his mother approved of this practical course. She was a hardheaded French provincial who berated her husband for his improvidence and countered his visionary advice to young Raymond and his two older brothers with the oft-repeated suggestion that it was "Far better to be envied than pitied." Apparently the boys heeded her advice, for all three became substantial citizens of the United States: Maximilian, Jr., as a banker; Georges as a surgeon; and Raymond as head of a firm with a gross annual business running into millions of dollars.

Raymond Loewy came to the United States shortly after World War I, during which both of his parents had died. One of his brothers, already in America, had promised to get him a job as an engineer with the General Electric Company if he should come to New York. Raymond, whose training had been interrupted by the war, went back to L'École de Lanneau, graduating in 1919. Then he left for America, taking with him his engineering degree, his captain's commission in the French Army, a handful of medals, and—nothing else. After he had paid for his passage he was so broke that when he was asked to contribute to a war relief charity social on the boat, he had nothing to give. He did a quick sketch of a beautifully dressed woman and contributed that. This sketch marked a turning point in his career, for it later sold at auction for $150. Loewy, amazed, decided to abandon engineering for the more lucrative field of fashion illustration.

The magazine *Vogue* provided Loewy with his first opportunity as a fashion illustrator. Later he worked for *Harper's Bazaar* and for New York department stores such as Saks Fifth Avenue, doing window displays as well as fashion advertisements. His illustrations were marked by an innovation that has since become an advertising cliché: the use of a simple figure strategically placed in a sea of white space. The device was extremely effective in advertising layouts; however, when Loewy tried to apply the technique to window display, he was not uniformly successful. Saks encouraged his experiments, but when he displayed a single mannikin in Macy's window, he was immediately fired. Macy, unlike Saks, depended upon a large volume of business and could not afford to sacrifice space for the added emphasis which Loewy's arrangement gained.

In 1926 Loewy was asked to redesign a printing machine for a manufacturer. He took the machine to his apartment and worked on it in his spare time. Modifying the machine considerably, he eliminated unnecessary parts and simplified others, thus making it easier to operate and to repair. This was his first attempt at industrial design, and both he and the manufacturer were pleased with the results. Abandoning advertising, Loewy went in for industrial design on a large scale, redesigning automobiles, office equipment, household appliances, and many other products. As he tells it, one job just led to another until, today, he spends much of his time warding off new business.

Loewy's first big commercial success in industrial design was the Coldspot Refrigerator, which he executed for Sears Roebuck and Company in 1934. A completely new departure in refrigerator design, the Coldspot eliminated the unsightly, dust-catching motor housing, which used to be on top of the appliance. Loewy concealed the motor housing in the base of the refrigerator. The design boosted Sears' refrigerator sales by over 135,000 units in three years and won first prize at the Paris International Exposition in 1937.

Loewy also won a gold medal at the Paris Exposition for his contributions toward improved transportation. The locomotives which he had designed for the Pennsylvania Railroad in 1934 represented a radical new approach to train design. Cumbersome smokestacks and antiquated cowcatchers were discarded. Projecting head-lamps and whistles were embedded in an enveloping metal sheath whose sleek contours covered the entire engine. This sheath lacked the 2000-odd rivets that studded old-time engines, for its seams were welded, presenting no obstacle to the rush of the wind over its streamlined surface. Attached to an old-fashioned string of block-like cars, Loewy's new engine would have been as ineffectual as a polished arrowhead on an untrimmed stick. So Loewy designed streamlined cars of gleaming metal that whistled along behind his locomotives like polished shafts from a well-strung bow.

Not content with improving the exterior of the train, Loewy went to work on the inside. Before he had finished he had transformed the traditionally dingy coaches, pullmans, club cars, and compartments. Even the dining car was affected. Indeed, one of the railroad traveler's main sources of irritation was eliminated, for Loewy designed non-spill coffee cups for his high-speed train. On a Loewy-designed train the traveler could save time . . . and his vest.

Railroads were not the only medium of transportation to receive Loewy's attention. The Greyhound Bus Lines called upon him for his help. After riding hundreds of miles on buses to determine what improvements could be made in their design, Loewy developed a spacious new three-level model with body-conforming seats, washroom, water-cooler, and clear-view compartment for the driver. Long-distance travel in such buses is not the torture that cramping seats and infrequent stops once made it.

Truck drivers also have benefited by Loewy's activities. When the International Harvester Company employed him to modify the design of their trucks, he incorporated many features that added to the comfort and safety of the driver. Such things as arm-rests and storage compartments for personal belongings and cross-ventilating provisions for the cab of the truck are Loewy innovations. So too is the support built into the seat to protect the battered kidneys of long-distance truckers.

After World War II, the first basic automobile design improvements were made by the Studebaker Corporation, following Loewy's suggestions. These improvements included: greater all-around visibility through an increased window area; the use of black light in the dash panel for safer night driving; and a more comfortable rear seat suspended between the axles rather than, in the traditional position, over the rear axle.

Studebaker called on Loewy again in 1962 to design a four-passenger car which was named the *Avanti*. Loewy's plans called for a car with a lithe, clean look inside; a recessed, fully instrumented, wood-paneled dashboard; control levers mounted on a console between the two front bucket seats; light control buttons mounted above the windshield; a sharply sloping hood, without grill or fins; and a body with a slightly indented midsection, "Coke-bottle fashion," as Loewy described it.

In explaining his departure from standard styles, he said, "Generally speaking, for years, automobiles have resembled oversized boxes rolling on wheels. The true objective should be an automobile with improved aerodynamic characteristics, an appearance to interpret these facts, and, above all, a high degree of quality in the finished product."

More recently, the New York City Transit Authority commissioned him to design a dramatically different subway car. In 1966, he came up with a car with a slanting, streamlined end, which emphasized soft lines and slightly rounded sides; wider doors and windows; easier-to-read signs; bright interior colors; stainless steel fittings; fluorescent lighting; and vandal-proof seats.

The transportation industry is not, of course, Loewy's sole interest. He has designed everything from lipstick cases to supermarkets. His clients have ranged from those who wanted a new label to put on a bottle (Roma Wine), to those who wanted him to redesign a chain of stores (W. T. Grant and Company). He has designed terminals as well as buses for the Greyhound Bus Lines. Streetcar firms and toothpaste manufacturers have engaged his services. He has designed housings for electric shavers (Schick), packages for cigarettes (Lucky Strike), and caps for pens (Eversharp). Some years ago he was employed to do all the designing—from soap wrappers to retail stores—for Great Britain's 500-unit, globe-girdling Unilever Company.

A few months after President Kennedy's assassination in November 1963, Loewy and his firm were commissioned by Postmaster General John Gronouski to design a commemorative stamp based on some preliminary sketches made by Bureau of Engraving and Printing personnel. The finished product, approved by Mrs. Kennedy and other members of the late President's family, was one of sixteen designs submitted by Loewy. Gronouski called it "the most carefully planned stamp in postal history."

Loewy is aware that other factors besides pure need create a demand for consumer goods. He lists three such factors:

1. the American urge to replace
2. the psychological compulsion to keep up with the Joneses
3. salesmanship.

He admits that as an industrial designer he exploits these three factors. *Never Leave Well Enough Alone,* the title of his autobiography, is a confession of the extent of his exploitation. He does agree that some products have progressed beyond the improvement stage. It would hardly be possible, for instance, to improve the design of the common needle. And he does observe some taboos. For example, when he was asked to help a builder of grave vaults, he declined, saying, "I cannot improve upon death." But the limits which he imposes upon himself are as few as his profits are great.

Perhaps the curious character and career of Raymond Loewy can best be disclosed by a final illustration. It concerns a $50,000 bet that Loewy proposed to the late George Washington Hill, tight-fisted head of the American Tobacco Company. Loewy's bet was that he could improve the green Lucky Strike package and that, as a result, Hill would sell more cigarettes, without changing their quality. His improvements consisted of a change in the package color, from green to white, on the theory that since people put cigarettes in their mouths they like to see them in a sanitary-looking container. He also discarded the printed matter that had occupied one side of the pack, reproducing the bull's-eye trademark on both sides. Thus when a smoker threw an empty pack away, the brand would be advertised, no matter which side of the pack was exposed. These two minor changes in package design and no change in the quality of the product brought a marked increase in sales. So Loewy won his $50,000!

Spyros Skouras

THE story of Spyros (pronounced Spear-o) Skouras'
life is almost as fantastic as the plot of one of the
forty-odd pictures which his Twentieth Century–Fox
Film Corporation produced every year. It began in the
year 1893 in Greece, in the small town of Skourohien, or
Skourasville as it would be called in America. The town
had been founded by Spyros' grandfather in 1830, during the Greek War of Independence against the Turks.
But the family did not prosper, for the small village on
the Ionian Sea was beset by "Mediterranean Worm,"
which ruined the vineyards. One year during heavy
rains the village dam broke, flooding the Skouras farm
and leaving it covered with sand and stones when the
waters receded. Panagiotes Skouras, Spyros' father, was
unlucky in another particular also: half of his ten children were girls for whom dowries had to be provided,
and one of his sons died in infancy.

Under these circumstances the four remaining sons
had to be put to work at an early age. Spyros, who had
been destined for the priesthood, at thirteen left school
for a job in nearby Patras. He worked as a printer's

helper and later as an office boy in an insurance and navigation company. His older brother Charles emigrated to America, hoping to mend the family fortunes in the land where the streets were paved with gold. He started work as a bus boy at the Jefferson Hotel in St. Louis. When he had risen to the position of bartender, at a salary of $8 a week plus $25 in tips, he sent passage money to Spyros and upon his arrival in St. Louis in 1910, got him a job as bus boy at the Planters Hotel. The following year the two boys sent for their young brother George. Demetrios, the eldest brother, remained in Skourohien to rehabilitate the farm.

In America, Spyros' sixteen-hour day began at 3:45 A.M., when he presented himself to Frank Balzar, the bartender of the Planters Hotel. Balzar was a patriotic and energetic individual who insisted upon Spyros' joining him in singing "The Star-Spangled Banner" at the start of each day to improve his English and display his patriotism for his new country. After this early-morning rendition of the national anthem, Spyros began his work. He broke up twelve large blocks of ice, half into lumps for highballs, half into shaved ice for cocktails. Next he swept up and prepared the place for customers who would begin arriving at ten o'clock. He then doubled as a waiter until four o'clock. In the evening he studied English, shorthand, accounting, and commercial law at Jones Commercial College. By the time he got to bed his feet were often so sore that patches of skin came off when he removed his socks.

Spyros studied at Jones Commercial College for two years. Later he took night courses at the Benton College of Law, because he understood the value of commercial law in the business career which he planned. During all this time he and his two brothers lived frugally, walking to work to save the nickel carfare and allowing themselves only an occasional Sunday afternoon's entertainment at the nickelodeons, the precursors of our moving pictures.

By 1913 the three brothers had accumulated $3,500 in their joint bank account. Being approached by three fellow Greek-Americans in search of capital, they put up $3,000 of their savings for a quarter interest in a new nickelodeon called "The Olympia." Soon, however, the new partners quarreled. The Skouras brothers, who had invested their profits from the new venture jointly, bought out the other three. In a short while they were able to buy another small theater. They were on their way to financial success in the entertainment world.

Spyros had become a citizen of the United States and, in 1917, with our country at war, he joined the U.S. Army. He was trained as an aviation cadet, but the war was over before he received his commission, and he saw no overseas service. When he was discharged from the Army, he returned to St. Louis and worked with his brothers upon the expansion of their theater holdings. By 1926 the brothers had an interest in almost every important St. Louis theater. They built a $6,000,000 building in which to house their Ambassador Theater, a showy movie palace of the type that was soon to dominate the American scene. After a brief war with Paramount, which Spyros won by enlisting the aid of a former customer at the Planters Hotel, they began nation-wide operations. The elaborate stage and screen shows that were "the wonder of St. Louis" were soon being developed by the Skourases in theaters throughout the country.

The hotel experience of the three brothers had taught them the importance of courtesy and service. They discovered that the "personal touch" was as important in a theater as in a hotel. As a matter of fact, the two older brothers insisted upon treating their customers so effusively that George, the junior partner and man of all work, once rebelled. "Listen!" he angrily told his brothers. "I will polish the brass. I will carry the film. I will sweep with the broom. But, by God, I won't smile all the time. My cheeks ache!"

Spyros, more pliant and affable than George, soon became the spokesman for the brothers in dealing with the public. Charles, the cautious patriarch, kept Spyros' grandiose schemes in check and held the purse strings. It was Charles who would decide when the family budget could stand the strain of new clothes, and it was he who led the expedition downtown for the purchase of three identical blue serge suits. It was Charles, too, who supervised the health of the group, insisting that his brothers consume quantities of fruit, cheese, olive oil, and yogurt, and working out with them regularly on the wrestling mat which he had installed in their quarters.

Charles's role as boss of the three brothers has often been exploited for economic reasons. A story is told of Spyros' having settled a contract with a film salesman for a high price. Upon conclusion of the deal, Charles walked into the office and was told of the cost. He immediately grew angry and shouted, "What! Spyros, you are trying to bankrupt us!" Spyros insisted that he had made a good deal, and the two brothers began to argue furiously. They pounded the table, tore open their ties, ripped their shirts, kicked the furniture, and shouted at the top of their voices, while the frightened salesman sat and watched.

Finally Charles screamed, "O.K. Mr. Skouras! I don't call you brother any more. Go back to Greece!" Then he charged from the office, slamming the door and breaking the glass.

Spyros, apparently overcome, turned to the quaking salesman and gasped, "See, I did my best." The salesman, thoroughly hoodwinked, signed a new contract with Spyros at a much lower figure. The episode, with minor variations, was frequently repeated.

Actually, of course, the brothers worked in close concert with one another. As a matter of fact, one of the secrets of their early business success was their interchangeability. At business meetings that sometimes lasted all day and half the night the brothers would often spell one another. With his opponents groggy from lack of sleep, one Skouras would slip out for a steam bath, a rubdown, and a nap while, unbeknown to the weary antagonists, a brother replaced him and continued the negotiations.

The Skourases were hard hit by the financial crash of 1929, but they soon bounced back. They bought up a chain of theaters cheaply and were soon making money on them. Spyros took over a bankrupt chain of movie houses in the West, and within three years he had them on a paying basis again. He helped to reorganize the Fox Film Corporation, recommending the amalgamation which resulted in the formation of Twentieth Century–Fox Pictures. Though Spyros gained nothing directly from this deal, the goodwill he won was important. In 1942 he was made president of the new film producing company. He continued to play an active role in the theater management end of the business until the antitrust division of the Department of Justice started its battle to separate the production and management functions of the film industry. When the dust of that battle settled, the legal connections among the Skourases were severed. But there was no severing the close family ties uniting Charles, who headed 550 theaters comprising the second largest chain in the country, George, who controlled seventy movie houses in the East, and Spyros, with a $250,000-a-year job as head of one of the largest film producing companies in the country.

Though Spyros Skouras used to see over three hundred films a year and believed, according to a friend, that movies were "the greatest civilizing influence since Christianity, the greatest educational influence since the invention of movable type, the greatest cultural advance since the age of Pericles, and the greatest agency for political stability since the Roman Empire," his own greatest contribution to civilization was made in a sphere far removed from that of the moving picture. It was he who was responsible for organizing and directing Greek War Relief when Italy and Germany invaded Greece and laid it waste in World War II. He helped to raise over $12,000,000 for food, clothing, and medical supplies for the sick and starving people of his native country. And he managed, in the face of an impossibly complex international situation, to get the warring countries involved in Greece to refrain from interfering with these supplies. In undertaking this enormous job, he acted purely from humane sentiments and not because of loyalty divided between the country of his birth and the country of his adoption. When he was told that a toast was to be proposed to King George of Greece at a luncheon he was to attend in London for Greek War Relief, he objected. "Tell them I don't want it," he said, "because I am an American."

The motion picture industry felt the impact of television for the first time in 1951. Competition with the home screen forced most large movie-making companies to curtail their own production and to act as distributors for independent producers. The big companies laid off most of their stars, camera crews, and studio personnel. Spyros Skouras, the Colossal Optimist, would hear of no such thing. He argued that the business of movie companies was to produce movies, not to distribute them. And for him, the "star system" was not dead. He coined a slogan, "Movies Are Better Than Ever," and invested heavily in a new wide-screen film technique designed to give audiences an enormous panoramic picture and a new illusion of depth which television could not duplicate.

But as if to hedge his bets against the future, he became interested in shipping in 1956, and bought two 32,000-ton tankers. Subsequently, he formed two shipping companies, Skouras Lines and World Wide Tankers, and a holding company, Admiralty Enterprises, which owned and controlled the other two. With his brothers, he also acquired control of Prudential Lines and began a systematic ship replacement program. Owning the first two almost completely automated ships built in the United States, Prudential Lines was able to offer in 1966 the fastest transatlantic cargo liner service.

Meanwhile, to prove his great faith in the old Hollywood "star system," he decided in the late Fifties to put all of Twentieth Century Fox's eggs into one basket and produced the most expensive, biggest, best, longest, most spectacular movie ever made—*Cleopatra,* with Elizabeth Taylor, Richard Burton, Rex Harrison, and a galaxy of other stars. The original estimate of costs was $15 million.

But the picture was dogged with ill luck, and the final cost came to $40 million. A large percentage of the film had to be scrapped and begun again after Elizabeth Taylor became sick. Her off-screen romance with Richard Burton produced world-wide headlines during the filming, most of them considered bad publicity. Profits dropped, no dividends were given to shareholders, for two years the company ran on a deficit and Twentieth Century–Fox's stock fell on Wall Street.

Finally, in May of 1962, Skouras faced three hundred angry stockholders at an annual meeting. He failed to convince them that *Cleopatra* would be a success. A group of Wall Street lawyers and financiers began manipulating behind the scenes to oust Skouras from the presidency. In June, during the company's longest and stormiest board of directors meeting, Skouras was forced to resign.

But the battle was not over. "Wall Street" was determined to show "Hollywood" how to make money out of the movies and to place one of their own men in the presidency as Skouras' successor. But Hollywood thought it was absurd to let Wall Street make movies.

From abroad, producer Darryl F. Zanuck, one of the founders of Twentieth Century–Fox and the company's largest single shareholder, announced he was going to take a much greater interest in how the company was run. At a showdown battle in July, Zanuck was elected president and Skouras was named chairman of the board.

Cleopatra finally opened on June 12, 1963. The four-hour spectacular met with mixed reviews by the critics. But the audiences must have loved it, for it finally broke even—and went on to make money.

Whether he was up or down, Skouras always maintained a boundless optimism best summed up in a telegram he once sent to a St. Louis theater owner who was having financial problems. Skouras wired, "No mariner ever distinguished himself on a smooth sea."

Alfred Hitchcock

Scene: A merry-go-round in an amusement park. Gay carousel music. Laughter. Children scampering about, choosing their favorite wooden horses for the ride that is about to begin.

Lights!   Action!   Camera!

A whirl of brightly colored horses round and round. Suddenly, guns blaze. The operator of the machine is hit and his carousel circles madly, out of control. Men run into the spinning circle, exchanging shots amid a swirl of screaming children and lunging wooden horses, while the music pipes gaily away.

Cut!   Stop the cameras!

The scene is marked by the unmistakable "Hitchcock touch," its carefully detailed background of gaiety counterpointing the stark horror of the action of the unfolding plot.

But let's follow the swinging boom of the camera to another imaginary set, for it is not alone in such dramatic contrasts as we see illustrated in this scene from

Strangers on a Train that the Hitchcock touch consists. It is rather in the skillful use of the camera to pick up and emphasize details significant for his purpose that Hitchcock excels. Observe, for instance, the classic example of fine camera work from the film *Foreign Correspondent.*

We are looking down from a balcony into a crowded, rain-drenched square. Beneath their glistening umbrellas, thousands of people stand, waiting expectantly for the appearance of a distinguished statesman. There is a flurry of activity as the famous man steps from a building. Photographers, shielding their cameras from the rain, kneel on the wet stones to photograph him. Bang! A shot sounds. The great man slumps to the ground. Dead. An enemy agent disguised as a photographer, his gun concealed in a camera, has assassinated the statesman. Now, from the vantage point of the balcony, we watch the agent's escape, his path revealed from above as our camera follows a disturbance through the mass of densely packed, glistening umbrellas.

Our position has enabled us to observe the escape. But more than that, it has pointed up the difficulty of detecting the fleeing man amid the obstacles at the scene of action. Again, the Hitchcock touch!

Having seen Hitchcock at work, let us use our make-believe camera for a flashback. The scene is London. The time, August 13, 1899. We are in the crowded, noisy streets of a market district. Our camera, panning, reveals stalls heaped up with fruits and vegetables and butcher shops with the bloody carcasses of slaughtered animals hanging in the windows. It comes to rest upon a sign:

WILLIAM HITCHCOCK, POULTERER

Inside the store beneath this sign the proprietor is weighing a freshly killed chicken for a customer. He pauses nervously, looking over his shoulder toward the back of the shop. Then he finishes his job and walks to the rear of the store. Opening a door, he listens expectantly. In a moment there is a loud wail from the upper story and William, still wearing his stained shop apron, dashes up the stairs. In the hall above he is met by an elderly woman who informs him that his wife, Emma, has given birth to a husky baby boy. Alfred Hitchcock has just been born.

Young Alfred grew up amid the noise and color of the London market district in which he was born. He was an independent child with a craving for adventure, and he soon began to roam far from home in his search for it. Before he had reached his eighth birthday he had ridden to the end of every bus line in sprawling London. And when, during his boyhood, his father became a fruit importer as well as a poultry dealer, Alfred began to dream of still more distant places as he helped to unpack the exotic fruits that came to the store from the far corners of the world. He visited the London wharves and the ships set him dreaming of adventures in strange lands. One wall of his bedroom he covered with a huge map of the world. On it he traced the courses of British vessels through the seven seas, getting his information from shipping reports in the daily papers. Already he was displaying that interest in adventure and in exact detail that was later to distinguish his films.

While at St. Ignatius College, the London secondary school which he attended, Alfred decided that he wanted to become an engineer. Upon graduating, he enrolled at London University, majoring in electrical engineering. Soon, however, he had to quit the university, for his father's business was failing and Alfred had to help support the family. His training helped secure him a job as a technical clerk in a London cable manufacturing company. Abandoning any idea of becoming an engineer, he nevertheless continued his education, studying economics and art at night. His developing artistic talent soon made him a valuable asset to the company for which he worked, and he was advanced to the advertising department. Designing advertising layouts by day and attending school at night, young Hitchcock satisfied his craving for adventure by spending his odd moments at the newly invented moving pictures.

Though Hitchcock soon became an avid movie fan, he was annoyed by the inartistic way in which the film titles were announced on the screen. The sloppily executed lists of credits also disturbed him. Using the titles of some of the films he had seen and filling out the list of credits with the names of friends, Hitchcock designed a series of title and credit cards that were artistically satisfying. Presenting himself at the newly opened London studios of the Famous Players Company, Hitchcock ran the gamut of doorkeepers, secretaries, and vice-presidents with his cards. Eventually he reached the head of the film company, who liked his ideas so well that he hired Hitchcock immediately, putting him in charge of the title department of the Famous Players Company. The year was 1920. Alfred Hitchcock's career in the moving picture industry had begun.

Hitchcock's first step toward the director's chair was taken a year or so later when he left the Famous Players Company for a job with Gainsborough Pictures. As a matter of fact, his new position with the smaller company involved several jobs, for he functioned as art director, script writer, assistant director, and production manager. But he was soon a full-fledged director, and it was in that capacity that he made his reputation, producing for Gainsborough, and later for Gaumont-British Films, moving pictures which helped put the British film industry on its feet.

One of the earliest films to reveal the authentic Hitchcock touch was a silent picture that he directed in 1926. Called *The Lodger,* it was a melodrama based on the exploits of Jack the Ripper, a notorious London murderer. In this picture Hitchcock used for the first time a device that was later to be identified with his name and that he himself came to consider "the core of the movie"—the chase. Skillfully employed, the chase gathers momentum in the picture as the terrified public and the police accumulate information that narrows the mysterious killer's sphere of operations. The action is largely psychological in the early reels, for the murderer is still unknown. But in the final reel, after a climax of tension has been reached, pent-up emotions are released in the swift movement of headlong flight and pursuit.

In *The Ring,* a silent film about a prize fighter that Hitchcock made in 1927, new film techniques that were to be exploited later with great success were introduced by the director. In one scene, for instance, the camera focuses upon a champagne glass in which the bubbly wine gradually goes flat while the elated young boxer waits in vain for his missing wife to return and celebrate his victory with him. The significance of the scene is thus revealed through the photography and not solely by means of dialogue or description, methods more appropriate in the theater and the novel.

Hitchcock called *Blackmail,* a picture which he made in 1929, a "silent talkie." Planned as a silent film with a view to conversion should the "talkies" prove to be practical, the sound was dubbed in after the picture was finished. The film was Hitchcock's first attempt at a "talking picture." In it he proved that the moving picture could assimilate human speech, the vehicle of the drama, without slavishly imitating the methods of the stage. He preserved the integrity of the film by continuing to emphasize the functional role of the camera.

For a time Hitchcock's principal interest lay in the adaptation of plays and novels to the screen. His most notable success with a filmed play was his movie version of Sean O'Casey's *Juno and the Paycock,* in which Barry Fitzgerald starred. Among the novels which he converted into movies were *Jamaica Inn,* starring Charles Laughton, and Hall Caine's *The Manxman.* These efforts helped pave the way for his skillful adaptation of Daphne Du Maurier's *Rebecca* into a film which won the Academy Award in 1940. His experiments convinced him, however, that the crime or spy melodrama provided the type of story that was best suited to the motion picture. His later films—with several striking exceptions—were largely confined to the exploitation of such stories.

Between 1935 and 1938 Hitchcock directed a cycle of six melodramas for Gaumont-British Films which have been described as "unquestionably his best work." These films were *The Thirty-Nine Steps* (based on John Buchan's thrilling story), *The Secret Agent, Sabotage, The Girl Was Young,* and *The Lady Vanishes.* Of uniform excellence, these pictures are still being shown as outstanding examples of film art. Commenting on the cycle, Lawrence Kane in *Theatre Arts* analyzed Hitchcock's distinctive contribution to the screen in the following words:

> The Hitchcock style could at last be clearly defined. It resulted in melodramas told against painstakingly realistic backgrounds, taut of plot and characterization. His cameras moved with sureness and suddenness rarely equalled. His lighting retained only the best of what the German innovators had developed in the last decade, stark but never sensational for its own sake. He had achieved that most difficult of ends: the construction of a believable world from insubstantial shadow.

Hitchcock's success in creating a believable world out of insubstantial shadow is largely the result of his painstaking attention to detail. Together with his wife, Alma, whom he married in 1926 when she was serving as his script writer and associate director, he plans out his scripts very carefully, hoping to follow them exactly when he starts to shoot. "In fact," says Hitchcock, "this working on the script is the real making of the film for me. When I've done it, the film is already finished in my mind."

The amount of effort that Hitchcock puts into a film before he begins to shoot can be illustrated by a comparison. The normal shooting script for a Hollywood movie consists of about fifty master scenes. A typical Hitchcock script is broken down into approximately six hundred numbered scenes, each complete with sketches of characters as they are to be grouped and with camera positions carefully noted. In addition, Hitchcock often furnishes the actors with dozens of his own lively sketches, illustrating the facial expressions he expects of them at various points in a scene.

It is not merely the amount of preparatory work, however, that determines the excellence of Hitchcock's best films. It is the result of the man's vision, of the appropriate use of means to secure a desired end. The procedure is best described in his own article, "Direction by Hitchcock" in *Footnotes to the Film,* when he says:

> What I like to do always is to photograph just the little bits of a scene that I really need for building up a visual sequence. I want to put my film together on the screen, not simply to photograph something that has been put together already in the form of a long piece of stage acting. This is what gives an effect of life to a picture—the feeling that when you see it on the screen you are watching something that has been conceived and brought to birth directly in visual terms. The screen ought to speak its own language, freshly coined, and it can't do that unless it treats an acted scene as a piece of raw material which must be broken up, taken to bits, before it can be woven into an expressive visual pattern.

When the procedure suggested here is followed by a man of Hitchcock's talent, the results are such fine films as *The Thirty-Nine Steps, The Lady Vanishes,* and *Foreign Correspondent.*

Hitchcock's great British movies brought him offers from Hollywood and, after an exploratory trip to the United States in 1938, Hitchcock returned to take up permanent residence here, lured by a contract which offered him $800,000 for five pictures. *Rebecca* and *Foreign Correspondent,* his first American pictures, were as fine as his best British films. The former picture, adapted from a best seller, dealt with a theme different from those which Hitchcock customarily handled. But anyone who recalls the entrance of Mrs. Danvers, as played by Judith Anderson in that picture, will realize that the director had lost none of his skill. In explaining that scene Hitchcock says, "Mrs. Danvers . . . upsets you because she comes suddenly from nowhere right into your consciousness. Had I built her one of those stately pedestrian entrances, your reaction would have been at once, 'Oh, here comes the menace. I'm not scared a bit.'" The explanation shows that Hitchcock was still thinking of the acted scene "as a piece of raw material which must be broken up . . . before it can be woven into an expressive visual pattern."

Foreign Correspondent was a great spy melodrama that confirmed Hitchcock's reputation as a master of suspense. The hard-working director put so much effort into the filming of this picture that he lost over thirty pounds while it was being made. Enormously stout, Hitchcock didn't mind the weight loss. He still had more than two hundred pounds left.

Up to this point in his career Hitchcock had not attempted a straight comedy. In 1941 he fulfilled his ambition to direct a typical American comedy about typical American people. The picture was called *Mr. and Mrs. Smith*. After producing it he returned to melodrama. But he was beginning to be affected by the unhealthy influence of the box office. His next picture, *Suspicion,* though it won an Academy Award for its star, Joan Fontaine, is marred by a compromise ending which destroys its artistic integrity. *Saboteur,* which Hitchcock directed in 1942, represents an attempt to cash in on his own reputation by imitating one of his early successes, *The Thirty-Nine Steps.*

Hitchcock redeemed himself somewhat in *Shadow of a Doubt,* a picture upon whose script he collaborated with the novelist Thornton Wilder. And his directing of *Lifeboat* showed courage, for the strongest character in the film is a Nazi U-boat captain. But his next three pictures reached depths of banality and bad taste only equaled by veteran Hollywood hacks. *Spellbound,* filled with conventional camera tricks, was "immensely undistinguished from an artistic point of view." *Notorious* was vulgar and trite. And *The Paradine Case* was, according to one admirer of Hitchcock, "the worst picture he ever made."

Some say that the famous fat man, who trademarks his pictures by appearing briefly in each of them, has not produced a picture in recent years that is worthy of that famous stamp. They fault him for refuting his own cinematic principles in such pictures as *Rope, Rear Window* and *Dial M For Murder,* where he shot scenes in very long takes, rather than in many short ones.

Several years before, Hitchcock had explained why short instead of long scenes result in better movies. "If I have to shoot a long scene continuously," he said, "I always feel I am losing grip on it, from a cinematic point of view. The camera, I feel, is simply standing there, *hoping* to catch something with a visual point to it."

In 1964 he produced *Psycho,* a film which has been described as pure horror. Notwithstanding some unfavorable criticism it apparently satisfied his audience: it made $15 million. Since it cost only $810,000 to produce, it has been one of the most successful movies ever made in terms of profit on original investment.

Hitchcock moved into television in the mid-fifties, while simultaneously producing motion pictures. His half-hour thrillers enjoyed a huge popularity, and are run and rerun. He appeared before, in the middle of, and after each show, with a sly dig at the commercials that delighted the sophisticated viewers, but sometimes made the advertisers angry.

In 1962 his television series was expanded to an hour. He told an interviewer in 1966, with tongue in cheek: "Violence on television is good for the soul. One of television's great contributions is that it brought murder back into the home where it belongs. Seeing a murder on television can be good therapy. It can help work off one's antagonisms. If you don't have any antagonisms, the commercials will give you some."

Hitchcock produced his fiftieth motion picture in 1966. Titled *Torn Curtain,* it unfortunately disappointed the critics and his admirers. The consensus was that it was an ordinary spy story, full of clichés and lacking in wit, imagination, and suspense.

Nevertheless, to celebrate it as Hitchcock's fiftieth film, New York City Mayor John V. Lindsay presented him with the city's bronze medallion of honor "for his achievements in the cinema arts." If his work is not up to what it used to be, Hitchcock has still earned a permanent place in the history of American culture. He gave a new dimension to movie-making, exploiting the potentialities of the camera as no one had done before him to create suspense and interest in the fates of the characters that flit across the silver screen.

Enrico Fermi

"THE Italian Navigator has reached the New World."

"And how did he find the natives?"

"Very friendly."

It was a strange way to announce the birth of the Atomic Age. But it was war time, and the project—the implications of which were that mankind could never return to simpler, easier times—was top secret.

The message was in code and it was sent by phone from Chicago to Boston on December 2, 1942. It signaled man's first controlled release of nuclear energy. It meant that the atomic bomb was possible. The project had opened the door of the universe and placed at man's disposal an unlimited source of power, with the awesome choice of total destruction or the creation of a new world.

The Italian Navigator, heading the team of scientists who delivered the biggest brain-child ever conceived, was Enrico Fermi.

Fermi was born in Rome on September 29, 1901, the last of three children born to Alberto and Ida De Gattis

Fermi in quick succession. Schoolwork was easy for Enrico, and he soon found himself interested in science. To satisfy his thirst for mathematics and physics, Enrico needed books that were not available to him in school. He found them in the book stalls of an outdoor market in Rome, where he read them and once in a while bought one.

An engineer friend of his father's became impressed with Enrico's talents and began giving him math and physics books of increasing complexity. Soon the boy's abilities outstripped those of his father's thirty-seven-year-old friend, who then encouraged him to apply for a fellowship at a special school in Pisa. Enrico won the fellowship when he was seventeen on the strength of a paper he wrote on vibrating strings.

At Pisa, Enrico again found classwork easy. With a new friend, Franco Rasetti, Enrico found time to indulge in the kind of hi-jinks young students have performed from time immemorial. Once, Franco and Enrico were almost expelled. They were saved only by the pleading of their physics professor who recognized their extraordinary talents.

Enrico was but twenty when he received his doctor's degree in physics. His thesis was on experimental work with X rays, and his oral dissertation was far above the heads of his eleven examiners.

A few months later, Fermi went to Göttingen in Germany to study with the prominent German physicist

Max Born. Born's class included Werner Heisenberg, one of the German scientists who would try later to develop an atomic bomb for Adolf Hitler. Fermi, the only Italian in the group, was not too happy in Germany and seven months later came back to Rome to teach physics at the university.

It was then he first met his future wife, Laura Capon. Laura was but a girl of sixteen and she was not impressed with the twenty-two-year-old physics instructor. The next time she saw him was two years later when Fermi spent the summer vacation with Laura and her friends. She found Fermi a true believer in physical exercise, and she was sometimes irritated with his inordinate pride in his own prowess and stamina. Enrico, always in charge of the group, would outrun, outclimb, and outsee everyone else on the long hikes they took through the mountains. But Laura came to accept his foibles, and they were married two years later on a scorching July day in 1928.

Fermi's first stay at the University of Rome as an instructor lasted a year. He then went to Holland for further studies, after which he taught for a while at the University of Florence. While in Florence, he worked out a mathematical system for describing and predicting the behavior of molecules in a perfect gas. His theory has proved useful in explaining thermal and electrical conductivity in metals.

Just after his theory was published in 1926, Senator

Orso Corbino, chairman of Rome University's physics department, decided Fermi was the man he needed to build up his department's reputation. Corbino, in his dual capacity as a university professor and a member of the Italian senate, convinced the faculty and government to create a new chair in theoretical physics. In line with custom, he held a competition among physicists for the coveted teaching post. As the senator expected, Fermi won. Corbino then induced one of Fermi's friends, Franco Rasetti, to join his department's faculty.

In a short time, the department's reputation began to grow and attract many talented students, from both Italy and abroad. Among the students were Edoardo Amaldi and Emilio Segrè, who stayed on with Fermi and Rasetti to form the nucleus of a researching, writing, and teaching team of physicists.

The four men worked well together. Fermi, who was considered infallible in his field—that is, he never made a mistake—was nicknamed "the Pope." Rasetti, who took charge in Fermi's absence, was called "the Cardinal Vicar," and Segrè's crusty temperament earned him the title of "Basilisk."

Segrè, describing Fermi's talents as a teacher, said: "He seemed like a steamroller that went forward slowly, but that nothing could stop. The final result was always perfectly clear, and one was often tempted to wonder why it had not been found long before, so simple and natural did it all seem."

In 1929 Enrico was named a member of the Royal Academy of Italy. It was quite a coup for Corbino's physics department; but Fermi always felt uncomfortable in the gaudy uniform academy members wore when they met and posed for pictures, especially with its feathers and sword.

In 1932 Fermi turned his exceptional mind to the problem of formulating what happens when a naturally radioactive nucleus disintegrates. Two years later, he published his *Tentative Theory of Beta Decay,* which firmly established his international reputation. Many scientists, however, disputed the complex ideas advanced in this paper and it wasn't until almost a quarter of a century later that delicate experiments proved Fermi right.

In 1934 Fermi became interested in an important announcement by two French physicists, Frédéric Joliot and his wife, Irene Curie. By bombarding aluminum atoms with alpha particles, they had created an artificially radioactive form of aluminum. Alpha particles are positively charged helium nuclei, which are the decay products of such naturally radioactive substances as radium. Spontaneously breaking down, radium emits pieces of itself, and some of the pieces are helium nuclei, or "alpha" particles.

The Joliot-Curies had directed some of these particles against aluminum and found that a few of the aluminum atoms became radioactive themselves and were, in turn, breaking down. The trouble with the Joliot-Curie bombardment method was that it was a hit-and-miss system. To make an aluminum nucleus radioactive, an alpha particle had to collide with it. Since both the nucleus and the alpha particle had positive electrical charges, they tended to repel each other. Furthermore, the electrons around an aluminum nucleus had negative electrical charges, which strongly attracted the alpha particle, slowing it down rapidly until it stopped altogether. The chances for an actual collision between particle and nucleus were therefore very slim.

Fermi theorized that those collision chances could be vastly increased—thus making it easier to produce artificial radioactivity—if a neutron, instead of an alpha particle, were used as the nuclear bullet. The neutron had been discovered as a part of the atom two years earlier by the English physicist James Chadwick. Neutrons have neither a positive nor a negative charge; so, Fermi reasoned, neutrons would be neither attracted by electrons nor repelled by nuclei. Their speed and energy would remain higher than that of the alpha particles, and the odds of a neutron hitting a nucleus would be much greater.

There was only one way of proving Fermi's theory. Fermi the theorist became Fermi the experimenter. Rasetti, Segrè, and Amaldi, joined by Oscar D'Agostino, a chemist who had wandered into their laboratory one day and stayed with the group, waded into the new project enthusiastically with their friend and leader.

Enrico, methodical as always, decided to bombard all ninety-two elements with neutrons, starting with hydrogen. The first eight elements failed to react to neutron bombardment. Then fluorine was shot by neutrons and Enrico's homemade Geiger counters began clicking away merrily. The fluorine had become radioactive. One by one, various elements that followed fluorine on the periodic table showed the same susceptibility, they became radioactive through neutron bombardment. In the end, the four scientists had created more than sixty kinds of radioactive nuclei—"Fermi atoms"—as they were called.

Fermi realized that, in most cases, when a neutron collided with a nucleus, the nucleus' atomic number increased by one. The substance became a different element, the next one on the Periodic Table. When they reached the last known natural element, uranium, whose atomic number was 92, Fermi deduced that he might be creating a brand-new element, not found in nature—element 93. One of the products of their actual experiment seemed to be this artificially produced element.

They published their speculations in a scientific journal in May 1934, not as an actual discovery of a new element, but merely as speculation. In June, Senator Corbino announced their findings in a speech and the Italian press, then completely under the domination of Mussolini's fascist regime, made a sensation of it, much to Fermi's embarrassment. Fermi and his group had never claimed the actual discovery of element 93.

Fermi found out five years later exactly what he had done. Otto Hahn and Frederic Strassmann repeated Fermi's experiment in Germany and after discarding many tentative explanations, concluded cautiously that from the uranium atom they had obtained radioactive barium. Lise Meitner, a brilliant woman colleague of Hahn and Strassmann who had fled Nazi Germany to escape the persecution of the Jews there, saw the implications. In Sweden Mrs. Meitner deduced what had happened: the uranium atom had split into roughly equal parts. Since the mass of the two parts was less than the total mass of uranium, she concluded that some of its mass had been converted into enormous amounts of energy.

In any event, Fermi and his team continued their experiments in 1934. One day, they were working with a piece of irradiated silver and noticed that it had different counts of radioactivity when placed in different locations in the room. They started interposing various substances between the neutron source and the silver and found that the radioactivity increased in different amounts. Then they tried paraffin. Geigers started chattering away in wild abandon. Paraffin had increased the artificial radioactivity of silver by more than one hundred times!

Fermi immediately went to work on a theory to explain the paraffin effect, and in a short while he had one. Paraffin contains much hydrogen, and hydrogen nuclei have the same mass as neutrons. Neutrons in going through the paraffin hit many hydrogen nuclei. They don't combine with the nuclei, but they do lose their speed. Slow neutrons would logically have a better chance of hitting silver nuclei and making the silver more artificially radioactive.

To test the theory, the men needed another hydrogen obstacle course for their neutrons. Water! They all rushed out to Senator Corbino's goldfish pond behind the physics building with their neutron source, their silver, and their Geiger counters. The theory was confirmed! Slow neutron bombardment was a fantastic source of artificial radioactivity. The slow neutron theory helped Fermi win the Nobel Prize in 1938.

The years between 1934 and 1938 were filled with routine teaching and experimenting. Fermi's reputation was assured, and as far as financial rewards were concerned, he was relatively comfortable. In 1936 Fermi's second child, a boy, Giulio, was born. His first, a girl, Nella, had been born in 1931.

Meanwhile, Mussolini's dictatorial hold on Italy was tightening year by year. At first, the Duce opposed the rise of Naziism in Germany. But then in 1936, he made a pact with Hitler, and the Rome-Berlin Axis was formed. That summer Mussolini imported anti-Semitism from Germany and issued Italy's first anti-Semitic laws.

For several years Enrico had watched the slow erosion of individual freedoms under Mussolini. He had not yet been touched as a scientist, a prominent one at that, but he felt it wouldn't be long before his teaching and research would be affected. As far back as the fascist march on Rome in 1922, Enrico had told his family that someday he would have to emigrate.

Sixteen years later, he knew that day had come. Laura was Jewish, and, although as the wife of a Catholic she was not affected by the anti-Semitic laws, Fermi did not want to live and raise his children in that kind of political atmosphere.

On November 10, 1938, Fermi received a phone call from Stockholm. He was told he had won the Nobel Prize in Physics! The Fermis went to Sweden with their two children in December, accepted the prize and, instead of returning as heroes to Fascist Italy, went on to the United States as political refugees. They arrived in New York on January 2, 1939.

Fermi took a teaching position immediately at Columbia University. Two weeks after their arrival, Fermi met Professor Niels Bohr, 1922 winner of the Nobel Prize in Physics, at a New York dock. Bohr came in great agitation over what was happening in Europe and what lay in store for his native Denmark at the hands of

Hitler. He told of Lise Meitner's explanation of what Hahn and Strassmann had done in Nazi Germany. In repeating one of Fermi's 1934 experiments, the German physicists had split the uranium atom.

Fermi's mind began working on the possibilities. It was probable that when the uranium atom was split by a slow neutron, not only energy was released, but neutrons were emitted as well. In ideal circumstances, if two neutrons were emitted, they would be available to split *two* other uranium atoms. If each of these atoms in turn released two neutrons, four would then be available to split four more atoms. In the next fission, eight neutrons would be released; in the next, sixteen, and so on.

This would be a self-sustaining chain reaction. And since each single fission produced energy, untold quantities could be released in a chain reaction. If man could control the release of such energy, atomic fission could become science's greatest boon to mankind during peace time. It could also provide the raw material for the world's most hellish weapon.

Once Fermi had expounded on the possibilities, it became obvious to many foreign-born scientists who had fled to America what sort of power Hitler would have at his fingertips if German scientists achieved the release of atomic energy. The United States had to be warned, had to be convinced that it should develop atomic power before Hitler did and had to make the commitment to produce atomic bombs.

Albert Einstein, the most prominent scientist in the

country, was recruited in the effort. He wrote a now-famous letter that was hand delivered to President Roosevelt in October 1939, explaining the possibilities. The President authorized the beginning of atomic research. But it wasn't until the day before Pearl Harbor that huge amounts of federal money were poured into the project of building an atomic bomb.

Meanwhile, Fermi at Columbia University and a new group of colleagues were experimenting with the chain-reaction theory. Two initial problems had to be solved: in fission, released neutrons traveled too fast, missing uranium atoms; and most of those neutrons that were produced escaped into the air or were absorbed by surrounding matter. Thus a chain reaction could not be achieved.

Fermi knew he could slow neutrons with water or paraffin, as he had done in 1934. After months of research, however, the scientists concluded that the hydrogen in water and paraffin absorbed too many of the neutrons to permit chain reaction.

For theoretical reasons, they decided to try carbon. They began piling layers of pure graphite blocks on top of each other. In alternating layers, lumps of uranium would be imbedded in some of the blocks. The contrivance was called an atomic "pile." Uranium and graphite were hard to come by until the United States made its full commitment to the project, which bore the code name, "Manhattan District."

Early in 1942, Fermi's project was shipped to Chicago. The pile he was building in the Columbia laboratory had reached the ceiling, with no results. A bigger place was needed. The government set Fermi and his men up in an unused squash court under the stands of the University of Chicago's football stadium, Stagg Field. There, the men had a 26-foot high room, 30 by 60 feet in area, in which to build their pile.

Small piles were constructed, experiments conducted, measurements made. Finally, in June, the scientists concluded with certainty that a chain reaction could be accomplished under a set of specific circumstances. The fast-moving uranium neutrons would hit the carbon atoms, slow down, and hit more uranium atoms. The only thing they did not know for sure was the exact critical size of the pile. If it was too small, too many neutrons might escape into the air instead of bombarding more uranium atoms. Great precautions had to be taken to keep the chain reaction under control.

It took several months for the government to ship all the necessary materials to Stagg Field. Some time in October, the men began building the huge spherical pile that would be needed. The floor and walls became black with graphite powder. The floor was extremely slippery, difficult to navigate across. The men's sweating hands and faces became so grimy they looked like coal miners.

Control rods of cadmium were built into the sphere. Cadmium absorbs neutrons to such an extent that only one rod was necessary to prevent a chain reaction. Three rods were built, one of which operated automatically: should the radioactive reaction go beyond a certain preset limit, this rod would drop automatically into the pile, thus stopping the reaction. Should the automatic rod fail, a second rod, operated manually by one of the scientists, would be pushed into the pile. The third rod, twenty-six feet long, was the master rod which would be pulled out bit by bit, while Fermi made his calculations. As a final precaution, three men would be perched on a platform above the pile, ready to flood the pile with a solution of cadmium, should the unexpected happen and the reaction get out of control.

Finally, on the evening of December 1, they reached what they thought was the critical size, somewhat earlier than they had expected. The sphere was not complete; the pile was flattened at the top and looked more like a doorknob than a sphere. All that remained was experimental proof that a self-sustaining chain reaction would be produced when the rods were pulled out, a reaction that could be controlled.

The $350 million experiment began the next morning. A pen had been connected with the Geiger counters and would automatically trace a line showing the intensity of radiation. Two of the rods were pulled out. Thirteen feet of the master rod were kept in the pile. Fermi directed the man operating the master rod to pull it out another foot. He predicted that the pen would trace a line that would go up to a certain point and then level off. The clicking of the counters increased, and the pen moved up. Calculations were made. The pen leveled off exactly where Fermi had said it would.

Little by little the master rod was pulled out, and each time the pen followed Fermi's prediction. Tension built up, as the forty people in the room watched Fermi manipulate his slide rule and give terse directions and as they heard the increased chattering of the Geiger counters.

Suddenly, there was what one participant described as "a sound like a thunderclap," at which "everyone stood stock still." The automatic control rod had accidentally fallen down into the pile and stopped the fission process. It was 11:35 A.M. Fermi broke the tension by saying, "I'm hungry. Let's go and have lunch." What has been called "the greatest experiment of all time" had to be interrupted by the habits of its methodical director!

According to some of those who were there, no one spoke of the experiment during lunch. They returned to the squash court at 2 P.M. and the experiment was resumed in small steps. At 3:20, Fermi gave another order, closed his slide rule, smiled and said the pen would now become "exponential," that is, it would now go up and up without leveling off and the pile would begin chain-reacting.

The rod was then withdrawn some more. As Fermi had predicted, the pile began to chain-react. The pen went up and up. It did not level off. The counters clicked away at an ever more rapid pace. Calculations were made, records drawn. Fermi let the pile operate for twenty-eight minutes. Then he shut it down by ordering the rods pushed in.

The Italian Navigator had reached the New World.

The next three years were spent in constructing the atomic bomb in utter secrecy. Enrico was assigned a bodyguard, as were some of the other prominent scientists working on the project.

Tens of thousands of people were engaged in working on various components of the bomb in Oak Ridge, Tennessee, Hanford, Washington, and "Site Y," which grew quickly from a boys' school on an isolated New Mexican mesa into Los Alamos, a city of six thousand people.

The Fermi family went to Los Alamos and lived in a barracks-like apartment house. A school was built for the children of the scientists who had been shipped there. "At great expense we have gathered on this mesa the largest collection of crackpots ever seen," is how General Leslie Groves, the Army officer in charge of the Manhattan District, was said to have affectionately described this galaxy of brilliant minds.

The atomic bomb was built in such secrecy that the wives of the scientists, including Laura Fermi, did not know until after it was dropped, August 6, 1945, on Hiroshima, Japan, just what their husbands had been working on.

After the war, Fermi and his family moved back to

Chicago. Fermi took a teaching and research position at the newly created Institute for Nuclear Studies at the University of Chicago, where he remained until his death some nine years later.

At the time of his death, Fermi was in the midst of a study of mesons which he had begun three years previously. Mesons are particles whose weight is somewhere between that of electrons and that of protons. Nuclear physicists believe the meson is the force or energy that keeps other atomic particles together, acting somewhat like a cement or mortar between building blocks.

Since receiving the Nobel Prize in 1938, Fermi had won several scientific and government awards, among them the Congressional Medal for Merit in 1946 and the $25,000 Atomic Energy Award on November 16, 1954.

Finally, shortly after his death, the one hundredth element, the eighth artificially created by man beyond the ninety-two that appear in nature, was named after him: fermium.

It turned out that Enrico Fermi was not wrong in 1934 when he speculated on the possibility of creating new artificial elements by bombarding uranium with neutrons! While his actual experiment resulted in the *fission* of uranium, the speculation that his experiment could create new elements was correct. It was left to other scientists—working feverishly on other aspects of the Manhattan District project—to confirm this and find the new elements.

In a memoir, Samuel K. Allison, one of the scientists with whom Fermi worked, called him "a man of really extraordinary intelligence and mental brilliance." Allison said Fermi "was perfectly well aware of his unusual mental qualities, but remained simple and unassuming . . . . In political matters, he was more to the right than most physicists, being quite skeptical of any extension of governmental powers which he believed might interfere with the possibility of each individual acting for himself. He habitually associated with young people and remained young in spirit throughout his life."

In his memoir, Allison lists Fermi's publications: nine books, more than one hundred and fifty articles in scientific journals and some seventy-five declassified reports released as documents of the Atomic Energy Commission.

Fermi's contributions to mankind will create a new world, if they are used for peaceful purposes. If they are used for waging war, man may completely destroy himself and his present world. The choice belongs to all of us.

The Italian Navigator, whose brilliant mind turned that frightening responsibility over to us, died of cancer on November 28, 1954, at the age of fifty-three.

W. H. Auden

WYSTAN Hugh Auden came from a relatively well-to-do family. He was born in York, England, on February 21, 1907, the youngest of the three sons of George and Constance Auden. His father was a doctor.

As a boy, Auden showed no inclination to writing poetry. His interests were largely scientific—photography, engineering, motorcycles and machines of all kinds. A good friend, Christopher Isherwood, noted that "his playbox was full of thick scientific books on geology and metals and machines, borrowed from his father's library."

Auden met Isherwood at St. Edmund's, a boy's preparatory school. Isherwood, who, many years later, would collaborate with Auden on a number of plays, remembered Auden as a "sturdy, podgy little boy, whose normal expression was the misleadingly ferocious frown common to people with very short sight" and who had "hair like bleached straw . . . . He was precociously clever, untidy, lazy and, with the masters, inclined to be insolent."

In his reminiscences, Isherwood said, "I see him boxing, with his ferocious frown, against a boy twice his size; I see him surpliced, in an enormous Eton collar, above which his great red flaps of ears stand out, on either side of his narrow scowling pudding-white face."

Auden himself was no less frank about his looks:

> *My head looks like an egg upon a plate;*
> *My nose is not too bad, but isn't straight;*
> *I have no proper eyebrows, and my eyes*
> *Are far too close together to look nice.*

—"LETTER TO LORD BYRON, PART IV"

If Auden's looks were distinctive, his conduct was often outrageous. He said of himself that he was "dishonest, sentimental, with no community sense whatever, in fact a typical little highbrow and difficult child."

His penchant for being different carried through all his young adulthood. His youthful rebellion against authority and accepted behavior is reflected in the harsh criticism of society that characterizes much of his early work.

As a boy, he steeped himself in the old Norse sagas, thrilling stories about Viking heroes, kings and gods, perhaps because his father made him aware of his Icelandic ancestors. Nevertheless, his interests were not primarily literary and he felt drawn to the modern mechanical life around him. In an autobiographical poem, written when he was thirty, he described this attraction:

> *But far better than any kings or queens*
> *I liked to see and know about machines;*

And from my sixth until my sixteenth year
I thought myself a mining engineer.

—"LETTER TO LORD BYRON, PART IV"

Auden might never have written a line of poetry, but for the chance remark of a boyhood chum, Robert Medley (who later became a painter and theatrical designer), when he was fifteen and attending Gresham School:

But indecision broke off with a clean-cut end
  One afternoon in March at half-past three
When walking in a ploughed field with a friend;
  Kicking a little stone, he turned to me
  And said, "Tell me, do you write poetry?"
I never had, and said so, but I knew
That very moment what I wished to do.

—"LETTER TO LORD BYRON, PART IV"

When he was eighteen, Auden went to Oxford University, where he again met Isherwood and showed his old friend the poetry he had been writing. Isherwood was very surprised to see Auden's work. He said, "People who understood machinery [as Auden did], I secretly felt, were doomed illiterates."

Isherwood rated the poetry as "extremely competent." Being a few years older than Auden, he became his mentor, criticizing lines and making suggestions.

Isherwood noted that his friend had lost none of his eccentricities: Auden "drank more cups of tea per day than anybody else I have ever known. Although this was the height of the summer, he insisted, if the day was cloudy, on having a fire in the sitting-room. At night he slept with two thick blankets, an eiderdown, both our overcoats and all the rugs in his bedroom piled upon his bed."

Some time later at Oxford, Auden met Stephen Spender, another poet. Spender recalled that Auden "regarded the university as a convenient hotel where he stayed and was able to read and entertain his friends." Nevertheless, according to Spender, "calling on Auden was a serious business. One made an appointment."

On one of these appointments, Spender remembered, "it was a bright sunny afternoon. As Auden hated daylight, all the blinds were drawn and the electric light was on. Auden wore a green shade over his eyes and looked like an amateur chemist."

Speaking of Auden's "fantastic fads," Spender said he "sometimes carried a cane and even wore a monocle . . . . Once he had been told by a doctor that he must walk as little as possible, so he immediately began going for 30-mile walks. He had a theory that the body is controlled by the mind."

Another writer-friend, Cecil Day Lewis, used to go for walks with Auden past the gasworks and the municipal rubbish dump. Lewis painted a word picture of Auden "moving with his phenomenally long, ungainly stride and talking incessantly, his words tumbling over one another in the hurry to get out, a lock of tow-coloured hair falling over the brow of his rather puffy but wonderfully animated white face. As likely as not, he was carrying a starting pistol and wearing an extraordinary black lay-reader's type of frock coat which came halfway down to his knees and had been rescued by him from one of his mother's jumble sales."

This, then, was the young man who was to become one of the most important poets of the age, and whose work would outrage both friendly and hostile critics.

It was Stephen Spender who privately printed Auden's first book of poems on a hand press in 1928, when Auden was still at Oxford and only twenty-one years old. The book has become a collector's item, since fewer than forty-five copies were printed.

The following year, Auden went to Germany. His parents had offered him a year abroad. He turned down France, because everybody went there, and Italy, because "Mussolini and Fascism made that impossible."

He picked Germany because "I knew no German and hardly any German literature, but, then, nobody else I knew did either . . . . Perhaps, also, I had an unconscious bias in favor of Germany because, when I was a little boy in prep school during the First World War, if I took an extra slice of bread and margarine, some master was sure to say—'I see, Auden, you want the Huns to win'—thus establishing in my mind an association between Germany and forbidden pleasures."

On his return, he settled down to five years of teaching and writing. During these years, he published several reviews, two volumes of poetry, a miscellany of poetry and prose called *The Orators,* and a play, *The Dance of Death.* The Orators is a satirical work dealing with the English public schools and attitudes toward war. In *The Dance of Death* Auden makes use of dancing, singing, a jazz orchestra, on stage and poetic parodies of popular songs to depict the decline of the middle class.

In 1935 he collaborated with the composer Benjamin Britten on a number of films, including the documentary classic, *Night Mail;* with John Garrett, on an anthology, *The Poet's Tongue,* and with Christopher Isherwood on a play, *The Dog Beneath the Skin.* The drama, parodying musical comedy, is about a man who is sent to find the missing heir of a village squire. He goes with a large dog, who turns out to be the missing heir in disguise. Their travels give Auden and Isherwood a chance to satirize the various classes of British society.

In 1936 he married Erika Mann, daughter of the famous German novelist, Thomas Mann. The Manns were political refugees from Naziism. Auden had never met Erika, but he married her in order to provide her with a passport to escape from a very troubled Europe.

In that same year, he traveled to Iceland with Louis MacNeice and wrote a book with MacNeice called *Letters from Iceland,* a collection of prose and poetic letters. He also wrote several pieces of criticism and another volume of poetry, *On This Island,* and he collaborated with Isherwood on the play *The Ascent of F6.* The play, in MacNeice's words, is "the tragedy of the man who gets his own way." It is about the attempt of a group of persons to scale a mountain known as "F6."

In the following two years, he went to Spain during the Spanish Civil War and, with Isherwood, to China, the United States, and Belgium. The trips resulted in more poetry; a record of their experiences in China, *Journey to a War,* and another play with Isherwood, *On the Frontier.* He also edited the *Oxford Book of Light Verse.*

His work in these years reflected his times, which were full of unrest. There was the Civil War in Spain, Benito Mussolini's fascist dictatorship in Italy, the rise of Adolph Hitler and Naziism in Germany, the great depression in the United States, the devastating effects of capitalism on workers in England. Young men all over the world were attracted to the promises of socialism and communism.

Auden himself was drawn to the left in politics, in reaction to Fascism and Naziism. Even in his early youth, he sympathized with the plight of exploited workers in the Midlands, a factory region of England.

In *Letters from Iceland,* he recalls what he saw in the Midlands:

> *Slattern the tenements on sombre hills,*
> *And gaunt in valleys the square-windowed mills*
> —"LETTER TO LORD BYRON, PART II"

Yet of that place of his youth, he says, "It's the most lovely country that I know," a reflection of his lifelong fascination with the big industrial cities of England and the United States.

Auden's friends were politically conscious, too, and sympathetic to the left. The circle of young poets and writers became known as "The Auden Group," and included Auden himself, Isherwood, Spender, C. Day Lewis, MacNeice and others. Auden's poem *The Dance of Death,* which forecasts a great upheaval of society, was so radical that he was mistakenly considered a communist. One critic says that the early Auden was a Cassandra reporting the breakup of society and predicting revolution and war, with a call to action to save the world.

In 1939 the storm clouds of war hung heavily over Europe, and many thought it would not be long before the storm would break out. The uneasiness and the changes, which Auden observed and commented on in his writings, would soon erupt into a world conflict that would forever destroy a past way of life and usher in a new age.

Disgusted with the peace-at-any-price compromise, which the British government made with Hitler at Munich, Auden left England and came to the United States. He became an American citizen in 1946. Why did he pick America as his new home? He told one interviewer:

"The attractiveness of America to a writer is its openness and lack of tradition. You are forced to live here as everyone else will be forced to live. There is no past. No tradition. No roots—that is, in the European sense. But what is happening here is happening everywhere."

How prophetic he was! Mankind has since struggled through several wars, scores of revolutions, and the shifting alignments of nations. Old forms have passed, traditions have died and there are few places on earth that have not had some of their roots pulled out by new sciences, new politics, new technology and new communications.

Auden's attraction to America's rootlessness is expressed in one of his poems, *Another Time:*

> *For us like any other fugitive,*
> *Like the numberless flowers that cannot number*
> *And all the beasts that need not remember,*
> *It is today in which we live.*

Not tomorrow, and certainly not yesterday. Yet, ironically, in his restless search for new and different ways in which to express his thought, Auden sometimes went back in time to old, discarded poetic forms, experimenting with terza rima, ballade, villanelle, sestina and the alliterative line, a line of verse in which most of the words begin with the same letter.

Since moving to America, Auden has published more than a dozen volumes of his own poetry. But he has also been a teacher, a critic, an editor, a librettist, an essayist, and a playwright.

He has taught at many colleges, including Swarthmore and Bryn Mawr in Pennsylvania; Bennington in Vermont; Barnard in New York City; and Smith in Massachusetts. Although an American citizen, he was appointed Professor of Poetry at Oxford University in England from 1956 to 1961.

Among the many distinguished librettos he has written is the one he composed with Chester Kallman for Igor Stravinsky's *The Rake's Progress,* a musical fable which has been called one of the two major operas of this century.

In 1958 a list of Auden's works included 28 collections of verse, 5 dramatic works, 19 librettos, lyrics, and other musical pieces, 4 works of creative prose, 39 works of criticism, 18 introductions to the works of other authors, and 170 articles and reviews. And since then, his output has continued unabated!

For his work, Auden has won several coveted prizes and awards. They include the King's Medal for Poetry, the Poetry Award of the American Academy of Letters, the Pulitzer Prize, the Bollingen Prize for Poetry, and the National Book Award.

Many critics consider Auden one of the most important poets of his time; yet many others take exception to certain aspects of his poetry. Some do not like him when he is flippant; some feel that the quality of his work is uneven; some find him obscure. One critic said, "In much of his work, scorn is the predominant note—scorn

of shallow emotion, philanthropic pretension, pluto-
cratic display, slickness, trite phrases, borrowed meta-
phors, sentimentality, secret vice—and these are things
which distract his attention when pure beauty is ready to
move him."

Auden's amazing variety of style is quite evident. He
can make such wry comments on the human condition
as:

> *In an upper room at midnight*
> *See us gathered on behalf*
> *Of love according to the gospel*
> *Of the radio-phonograph.*
>
> —"THE LOVE FEAST"

Or, with tongue in cheek, he might give such advice
as:

> *Thou shalt not live within thy means*
> *Nor on plain water and raw greens.*
> *　If thou must choose*
> *Between the chances, choose the odd;*
> *Read* The New Yorker, *trust in God;*
> *　And take short views.*
>
> —"UNDER WHICH LYRE"

Yet Auden can write truly poignant lines:

> *Never hope to say farewell,*
> *For our lethargy is such*
> *Heaven's kindness cannot touch*
> *Nor earth's frankly brutal drum;*
> *This was long ago decided,*
> *　Both of us know why,*

Can, alas, foretell,
When our falsehoods are divided,
What we shall become,
One evaporating sigh

  . . . I

—"THE SEA AND THE MIRROR"

And he can evoke disturbing feelings:

Dear, I know nothing of
Either, but when I try to imagine a faultless love
Or the life to come, what I hear is the murmur
Of underground streams, what I see is a limestone
landscape.

—"IN PRAISE OF LIMESTONE"

Many critics have noted Auden's progress from a general preoccupation with socialistic ideas in his early years to a profound commitment to Christianity later on. He was brought up as a High Anglican by his deeply religious mother. At the age of six, for instance, he had been a "boat-boy" at religious services, that is, he carried a bowl of incense that would be sprinkled by the minister onto glowing charcoal in censers.

But by the time he was a teen-ager, he had lost all his religious beliefs. Later, he sought ultimate meanings in psychology and radical political ideas. In the forties, the musician Igor Stravinsky recalls that he "was puzzled at first by what I took to be contradictions in his [Auden's] personality. He would sail on steady rudders of reason and logic, yet profess to curious, if not superstitious, beliefs—in graphology, for instance . . . in astrology, in the telepathic power of cats, in black magic . . . in categories of temperament. . . in preordination, in fate."

But gradually, Auden was coming back full circle to a preoccupation with Christianity. He has been criticized by some for his "shifting" views, and especially for abandoning his early interest in politics. But more recently, critics have recognized that Auden's "shifts" have not been capricious, that they represent a consistent progress of thought toward conservatism and a religious outlook.

One of his most sensitive works is *For the Time Being, A Christmas Oratorio,* in which he tries to harmonize the often contradictory elements of secular and religious experiences. In the poem Auden retells the story of the birth of Christ in modern language, building up to a climax that is followed by the post-Christmas letdown, as Auden sees it, the tough buckling down to meet the humdrum challenges of reality:

> *In the meantime*
> *There are bills to be paid, machines to keep in repair,*
> *Irregular verbs to learn, the Time Being to redeem*
> *From insignificance. The happy morning is over,*
> *The night of agony still to come; the time is noon:*
> *When the Spirit must practise his scales of rejoicing*
> *Without even a hostile audience, and the Soul endure*
> *A silence that is neither for nor against her faith*
> *That God's Will will be done, that, in spite of her*
> *   prayers,*
> *God will cheat no one, not even the world of its triumph.*

On the actual work of writing a poem, Auden once told a group of newspapermen:

"You begin to have an idea about something, and it mills around your head for months. Then it crystallizes and develops a kind of texture. You write it down in longhand. Then you type it, and it looks so awful."

When one of the newsmen asked him how long it took to finish a poem, Auden quoted another poet, Paul Valery, "A poem is never finished; it is only abandoned."

Contrasting the influential position of the ancient poet with the sad state of the modern poet, Auden acknowledged that poetry makes no money, either for the poet or his publisher. When he received the National Book Award in 1956, he expressed gratitude for the fact that publishers did keep on printing books of poetry, even though such books were financial losses.

Craggy-faced, his clothes untidy, his hair unruly, Auden accepted the award graciously and then told the men and women of the book industry:

"But what, in the name of profit, dear foolish publishers, kind unworldly booksellers, am I doing here, out of whom you know as well as I you will never make enough to pay the wages of one incompetent typist. I can only suppose that something inside you whispers that poetry has some value when common sense and your accountants tell you that it has none . . . . For your award, ladies and gentlemen, my thanks; for the dollars I shall never bring you, my apologies."

Erich Leinsdorf

Artur Bodansky was in charge of the Metropolitan Opera company's German repertory. He happened to be America's foremost Wagnerian conductor. Just five days before the gold curtain was to go up on the Met's 1939–40 season, Bodansky died and the company's directors had to find a replacement for him at once.

They called in the man who had been Bodansky's assistant for the previous two years, young Erich Leinsdorf, and asked him if he could shoulder the burden of rehearsing the cast and orchestra and of conducting the performances of the entire repertory of Wagner's operas.

Leinsdorf was only twenty-seven years old at the time and relatively unknown. However, he was anything but timid, and he said yes willingly. He had already proved himself to a small part of the public and to a few critics as a conductor with an extraordinary memory, a brilliant musical intelligence, and a prodigious appetite for hard work.

Yet all these qualities meant little to certain people at the Met, who wanted someone else, someone more experienced, more able to adjust to the musical and personal idiosyncrasies of the stars. At twenty-seven, Leinsdorf was considered a whippersnapper. After all, Bodansky was sixty-one when he died, and it had taken him years to gain the eminence he enjoyed.

A few weeks went by and while Leinsdorf's and the cast's performances won uniformly good reviews in the new season, the rumbling backstage grew louder. Finally, it fell to tenor Lauritz Melchior to voice the objections of the performers.

"He [Leinsdorf] is a musical genius," Melchior told a New York *Herald Tribune* reporter. "I have no doubt of it. But he is not yet ready to be senior conductor of the finest department of the greatest opera house in the world."

In the uproar that followed publication of the story, Edward Johnson, the Metropolitan's general manager, said, "There are some old boats in the company. There are those who, because they have exalted egos since they have no competition for their roles, would like to be dictators of the Metropolitan . . . . A small group is trying to gang up on a young man with a brilliant future. He will be so acclaimed in a few years that they won't want to remember that they opposed him. That's how much I believe in him. I'll stand before the world on that prediction."

Melchior retreated, telling a *New York Times* reporter that it was all "a tempest in a teapot caused by a series of misquotations" by the *Herald Tribune* and the feud subsided. A few days later, Johnson, Melchior, and Leinsdorf shook hands on the Metropolitan stage and Johnson said to the audience, "See, this is truly a house of harmony."

Leinsdorf never defended himself publicly, always refusing to give a direct answer to the accusation that he was too young and inexperienced. Later, he said of the bitter attack on him, "Any artist who faces the footlights one way or the other is open to criticism. It is up to the audience to judge, and all judgments, good or bad, are essential to reach one's artistic maturity."

It was a characteristic comment, made near the beginning of a musical career that took Leinsdorf all over western Europe and America before he reached the pinnacle he now stands on—the podium of what some critics say is the finest orchestra in the world, the Boston Symphony Orchestra.

Erich Leinsdorf was born in Vienna, Austria, on February 4, 1912, the son of Ludwig and Charlotte Loebl Leinsdorf. His father was an accomplished amateur at the piano, but he died when Erich was only three. His mother started him on the piano when he was seven. At ten, he says, he first began to see some meaning in music, as he was leafing through his father's old music books. It was no longer a matter of just learning a series of notes, but of understanding the relations among the notes, seeing the structure of the whole piece, determining how it was put together by the composer, knowing the piece almost as a living unity, a beautiful organism. It was this exercise of musical intelligence that shaped his tastes, that became his hallmark as a conductor.

At age thirteen, he added cello, musical theory, and composition to his studies. But then, he says:

"When I was seventeen years old, I stopped studying the piano as a means of working toward a musical career. My teacher . . . demanded an explanation of why I was stopping, when he had set such hopes in me as a future concert artist. I explained that I simply could not bear the hours of practice necessary in order to bring the stupid muscles of my hands up to the demands which the modern age required of the technical ability of the concert pianist."

And so, he decided to become a conductor.

He studied for a year at the University of Vienna, was dissatisfied with the music department, and enrolled at the Vienna State Academy of Music. As a scholarship student, he ran errands, copied music, and did other chores, as well as study.

He graduated in 1933, made his debut as a conductor in Vienna, and took several small posts, among them, assistant conductor of the Vienna Workers Chorus. The following year, he decided to apply for work at the annual Salzburg Festival, which was then under the direction of the famous conductors, Arturo Toscanini and Bruno Walter.

He had no money, so he hitchhiked one hundred and fifty-five miles to Salzburg. Arriving tired and dusty, he went into the Festspielhaus where Walter was at the piano rehearsing an opera scene. Walter interrupted himself at one point to walk over to a singer with some advice. One account has Leinsdorf deciding at that moment, "Now or never"; stepping up to the piano; and picking up the music from memory exactly where Walter had left off.

Walter was so impressed with his musical memory that Leinsdorf, at the incredibly young age of twenty-two, became assistant to Toscanini and Walter for the festival not only of 1934, but also of 1935, 1936, and 1937!

Between festivals, he worked as Walter's assistant at the Florence Music Festival; toured France and Belgium as a guest conductor; and spent two seasons working with Italian opera companies in Bologna, San Remo, and Trieste.

In 1937 word reached Toscanini that Artur Bodansky was ailing and needed someone to help him rehearse the Metropolitan Opera's Wagnerian cast. Toscanini recommended Leinsdorf for the job and the young man came to America. He wasn't expected to do much conducting. Basically, the job called for rehearsing segments of operas with groups of singers and doing chores for the great Bodansky.

But Bodansky could not conduct the performance of

January 21, 1938, and it was on this night—just two weeks before his twenty-sixth birthday—that Leinsdorf made his American debut, conducting Wagner's *Die Walküre*.

Lawrence Gilman, the New York *Herald Tribune* reviewer, described Leinsdorf in his review the next morning as "an astonishingly boyish figure." Gilman wrote: "Though he wiped his brow occasionally with his handkerchief . . . he soon made it evident that he was entirely at home in the great work before him and that he possesses an exceptional gift for eliciting its substance from the players under his command."

Three months later, Leinsdorf was called in an emergency to conduct an Easter performance of Wagner's *Parsifal*—a work of huge dimensions in both time and substance—on only twelve hours' notice! The next day, Gilman called the performance "one of the finest that has ever been heard at the Metropolitan."

That first season at the Metropolitan, Leinsdorf conducted ten performances. In the 1938–39 season, Bodansky fell ill more and more, and Leinsdorf conducted thirty-six performances. When the season was over, he took stock of his life, found he was in love with Anne Frohnknecht and married her on August 3, 1939.

Not too long afterward and three weeks before the 1939–40 season, Bodansky fell ill for the last time and died five days before the opening. Young Erich Leinsdorf took over, survived the backstage politics, and stayed as the Met's chief conductor of German operas until 1943. Between seasons, he appeared as guest conductor of the NBC Symphony Orchestra, the Montreal Orchestra, and the San Francisco Opera. In 1942 he became a United States citizen.

Leinsdorf left the Metropolitan Opera company in 1943 to succeed Artur Rodzinski as musical director and conductor of the Cleveland Orchestra. *Newsweek* magazine recalled that his conducting of the Cleveland Orchestra was so vehement, his wife had to sew his shirt cuffs to his jacket sleeves.

At the age of thirty-one, he was the youngest man ever to head a major American symphony orchestra. He was there but a month when he was drafted into the United States Army. Eight months later, he was released as a corporal on a medical discharge. Unfortunately, the Cleveland position was gone when he returned.

From then on, his musical career "meandered," as one critic put it, instead of going straight up, as it should have done for a man of Leinsdorf's great talents. For four years, he acted as guest conductor at various places, including the Cleveland Orchestra and the Metropolitan Opera, filling in during emergencies. In the middle of this period, in 1945, he was awarded an honorary Doctor of Music degree from Baldwin-Wallace College in Ohio.

But there was no permanent position available for

him until 1947, when he accepted the post of musical director and conductor of the Rochester Philharmonic Orchestra. He stayed there nine years, enriching the musical life of the city and working with the Eastman School of Music.

"It turned out to be less minor league than I thought it might be," he said of that period. "Some recordings we made there in 1952 and 1953 bear witness that one could get somewhere with an orchestra like that."

For his "extra-curricular" help in forming the Rutgers University Choir in New Jersey, Rutgers awarded him a Doctor of Music degree in 1952.

In 1956 he answered a call from the New York City Opera, becoming its director. The year was a financial catastrophe for the company. One critic called it "a disastrously overimaginative season of contemporary works." Leinsdorf produced the American premieres of Carlisle Ford's *Susannah,* Carl Orff's *The Moon,* and Frank Martin's *The Tempest.* The works were apparently too contemporary for New York's opera audience.

In his defense, *New York Times* critic Howard Taubman said that Leinsdorf "has a progressive orientation and is willing to take risks. The failures may be resounding, but they are preferable to tame routine."

Leinsdorf himself says that even though the season was a financial failure, it helped to convince private foundations of the need for subsidizing contemporary opera productions.

The next year, he returned to the Metropolitan as conductor and music consultant, a newly created position. He stayed with the Met for five years, producing, among other works, the American premiere of Verdi's *Macbeth* and the first performance since 1945 of Wagner's complete *Der Ring des Nibelungen* cycle.

An illustration of his enormous capacity for hard and varied work is the fact that during this period he was guest conductor for the Philadelphia Orchestra, the Boston, Pittsburgh, and London Symphony orchestras, the Los Angeles, Berlin, Vienna, London, and Israel Philharmonic orchestras, and the Vienna Opera. He was on the advisory committee for the new Metropolitan Opera House in Lincoln Center for the Performing Arts. And he made literally hundreds of recordings, including the complete set of Mozart symphonies and a dozen operas. His recording of Puccini's *Turandot* is one of the best-selling opera albums of all time and was cited by the National Academy of Recording Arts and Sciences as the 1960–61 season's best operatic work. His 1962 version of Wagner's *Die Walküre* won the *Saturday Review's* critics' poll award as the top opera recording of that year.

By this time, word was out that Charles Munch was going to retire as musical director and conductor of the Boston Symphony Orchestra. Four of five world-famous conductors vied for the post. Any guest conductor was automatically under consideration. When the decision was made, Erich Leinsdorf came out on top.

What was needed was not only the keenest musical intelligence, but also a director who could handle the Symphony Hall concerts, the orchestra's tours, the Berkshire Festival at Tanglewood in Lenox, Massachusetts, and the three-hundred-student Berkshire School. The conducting alone involved one hundred concerts a year.

Leinsdorf is the orchestra's eleventh conductor in its existence of eighty-seven years and only its third conductor in the preceding thirty-eight years. Munch had been there thirteen years and before Munch, Serge Koussevitsky had honed and refined the orchestra for twenty-five years.

There were a few off-key notes among the critics. Harold Roger, of the *Christian Science Monitor,* wrote: "Superb, but not superlative. There is no gainsaying that he [Leinsdorf] has done wonders with the orchestra, that he has refined its tone, adjusted its balance, polished its timbres. Yet, in nearly everything he does . . . his intelligence holds a slight edge over his emotions. For the finest and greatest music making, of course, the heart should hold a slight edge over the head."

After his first season (1962–63) in Boston, *New York Times* critic Harold Schonberg wrote: "Already in the space of one season, [Leinsdorf] has made the Boston Symphony a more precise group . . . . Few musicians would deny that he is a steadier conductor than Munch. There is, however, a touch of pedanticism in his work. Perhaps this is purposeful . . . . Greater freedom and more imagination may come as the years roll along."

Leinsdorf himself recognized some of this. Writing in 1964 about virtuosity in another connection, Leinsdorf said, "Let us put technique in its proper proportion. Sheer virtuosity is not enough. Technique, formidable as it may be, is not an end unto itself, but rather a means to a greater end. Technical virtuosity is not necessarily conducive to sensitivity and musicianship."

When Leinsdorf went to Boston, most other critics and musicians were far more enthusiastic than Roger or Schonberg. In his first months as leader of the Boston Symphony, he brought the orchestra to New York for a guest appearance during the opening week of New York's new Philharmonic Hall. Said the critic for *Time* magazine: "Few who listened doubted that one of the most distinguished eras in the orchestra's history had begun."

Life magazine said later, "Perfection is his passion. Leinsdorf has made his gemlike orchestra one of the finest ornaments of American music."

"I am in heaven when I play with him," said pianist Artur Rubinstein.

After Leinsdorf's first season at the orchestra's summer home, Tanglewood, ended in August 1963, bass clarinetist Rosario Mazzeo, who was then the orchestra's personnel manager, said, "His time is laid out by an IBM computer, but he's available to everybody. He could manage General Motors. The orchestra has enjoyed his easy way; we've had more fun this summer than we've ever had before." Eight months later, Mazzeo told *Newsweek* that the musicians "adore" Leinsdorf, adding, "Ours is the happiest orchestra in the world."

At Tanglewood, he amazed everyone with his phenomenal drive—breakfast at eight, mornings of rehearsals and teaching classes, afternoons of conferences and more rehearsals, evenings of performances. That first season, he conducted a Mozart series, a Prokofiev cycle and thirty-two works new to Tanglewood.

On March 31, 1964, he took the orchestra to the White House for the first time. Afterward, he outlined for an interviewer some of his thoughts about the Boston Symphony: "I want it to be a repertory orchestra. My men are at home with the familiar works, with the 'roast beef' like Beethoven and Brahms. Because of this, we free valuable rehearsal time for new works like the Benjamin Britten *War Requiem* or the *Kaddish* of Leonard Bernstein. I don't want the Boston sound. I want many Boston sounds. The sound of an orchestra should be like the costumes and gestures and speech of a great actor who plays King Lear one day and Big Daddy the next."

He explains his Wagner reputation this way: some men are born to Wagner, some achieve Wagner, and some have Wagner thrust upon them. Leinsdorf says he had Wagner thrust upon him.

"Ever since I moved to Boston," he says, "to conduct symphony concerts exclusively, one of the principal questions put to me in interviews is, 'How much do you miss opera?' Mind you, not, 'Do you miss opera?' because the questioner takes it for granted that it is impossible for one who conducted so much opera to live without it, but 'How much?' Half-seriously and half-facetiously, I reply that my nostalgia at this stage . . . is still controlled."

Leinsdorf has amazed his own men and other musicians with his remarkable gift for making a new work a complete part of himself. Once he had scheduled Walter Piston's *Symphony Number Seven*. He rehearsed it with the orchestra for the first time purely from memory. After the performance itself, Piston said in astonishment, "I wasn't prepared for a man to know my score better than I did."

Leinsdorf has a high regard for American music and American musicians. Of pianists, he says: "Dozens and dozens of the young Americans prove that we are approaching an American era in piano music. Many of these artists, all under forty and some only about twenty, have developed a brilliance of technique that still dazzles European concert-goers and critics while it is taken for granted as a necessity by American audiences . . . . These young Americans, having conquered the technical problems, are free to concentrate on the deeper and fuller meaning of the music they interpret."

Of critics, he says: "The significant music critics in the United States exhibit far more discerning taste and a much greater incorruptible objectivity than most of their European colleagues."

Leinsdorf doesn't mind adverse criticism. He says: "There are three worlds of music—the composer's, the performer's, and the critic's. I believe in friction, for without friction, there can be no progress. The music world cannot live without it."

Of his own field, he says, "Conducting is a matter of knowing that there is much you don't conduct. It's constantly alternating between listening and leading. Beating time is not conducting an orchestra."

Leinsdorf is a short, wiry, bald man. He has bright eyes and a mobile, expressive face. He and his wife, Anne, have five children: David, Gregor, Joshua, Hester, and Jenny.

Always meticulously dressed, he is an amateur photographer and collects stamps, wines, and mechanical toys. He reads history and enjoys the *Congressional Record*. "Where else can you find out exactly what is going on in this country?" he explains. "I especially look for Wayne Morse. What a maverick!"

From his children, he has developed a taste for jazz, with this qualification—"highly intricate jazz and *not* too loud."

Index

271